I OWE MY LIFE TO JESUS
-- YOU ALSO?

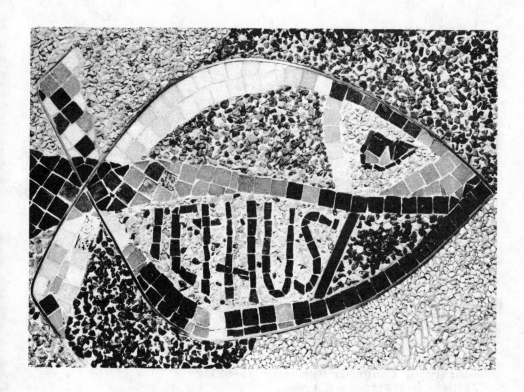

May the Lord shine upon Thee and give thee peace
H. Winky Lotz

by

H. WINKY LOTZ

Willyshe Publishing Co., Inc.
Linthicum Heights, Md.

Library of Congress Number - 79-92312
ISBN - 0-936112-00-X bound
ISBN - 0-936112-01-8 paper back

Published by
Willyshe Publishing Company
112 Mountain Road
Linthicum Heights, Md. 21090

I owe my life to Jesus -- You also?

Introduction:

Galatians 3: 23 - 29

...you are all sons of God by your faith in Christ Jesus ... There is no room for Jew or Greek, Black or White, there is no room for male and female; you are all one in Christ Jesus.

Dearly beloved, this is written to give you courage: Jesus is living! It is up to you to give him a chance in your every day life. Any decision you are making which you would, Your Lord rather not see -- forget about it, it is not worth your breath. If you **Owe Your Life to Jesus**, you owe him your trust and confidence also.

YES, if you owe your life to Jesus, there are also restrictions, there are a lot of things you cannot do without making him grieve. You cannot abuse yourself, your body and your mind. Believe me, you will be happier without drugs, prescription or otherwise, smoke, or alcohol.

Don't treat children like a necessary encumberance, nurture them, give their minds something to feed on while they are little. Don't let them pick up your bickering in their sleep. Everything children handle and investigate is for them an adventure, give them something to remember! Start discovering the world with them and through their eyes, like the Father in Heaven lets us discover his world through our eyes.

Talk to the Lord when you are happy, and when you are sad; let him know when you are neither ... when you are wretched talk in tongues ... that is when you give HIM a chance to overrule your ego-barrier. Don't ride your opinion until it is threadbare; if it is good for yourself, it might be detrimental for the other ... never forget that, while you are riding your opinion, you can't listen to the Lord.

When my mother let her temper fly, her uncle would tell her: "Martele, I would like to hear you sing, you do have a lovely voice." It was sincere and true, and she liked to humor him. Once she was singing all her frustrations evaporated and she could be the person, she wanted to be.

=1001=

I owe my life to Jesus--You also?

You and I are no different, we are frustrated in our shortcomings and insufficiencies to fully develop into that being we aspire to be. Christ knows that. All the cover-up cannot bluff HIM. No matter what you do, you cannot hide before the Lord. There are things you do for the body, and things you do for your soul. The former is necessary like good housekeeping, but you know you could, or would do rather without. But even if you'd live to 90 years of age, you know you will never be done with housekeeping. Don't make it the essence of you being. Christ gives you the purpose for you existence.

Whatever you do, do it for Jesus Christ as best as you know how. Create a happier family, starting with those you come in everyday contact. Change you image!

How do you do that? #1 Talk to the Lord, He does not mind, even if it does not make sense, He will drop you hints and ideas until you can formulate it. Then #2 talk about it to those you depend on and those you love, until it makes sense to them. Then #3 show them that you can stick to your program. #4 get all involved, and let them have the credit. I'll tell you it works. You get the cake, you get to eat it, and have a party to top it all. This is a prescription for every teacher ... who minds if the pupil gets further than the teacher? That is the most essential purpose of a teacher. Now, don't forget that we are all teachers, with or without a license, stepping stones for others to reach higher. Are we truly doing our job?

If we believe, if we have faith in Jesus Christ, if you owe your life to Jesus, HE gives us a value which is far greater than all the "garbage" we are carrying around. You don't preach because you are smart enough to figure out what other people want to hear, but because your heart runs over and you must share its abundance. If you are enthusiastic, be it not because you know how to be a good sales person, but because that is where your heart is. If you cheat on this, you cheat yourself most ... that is for what the devil is waiting.

What is in these pages is an attempt to share with you how Jesus Christ delt with me all my life, and to remind you to give him a chance for input.

Live, by the grace of Jesus Christ your Lord!

I owe my life to Jesus--You also?

IN MEMORY
        of my beloved ones, foremost of my dear mother and father, Aunt Johanna, Mary, Elizabeth and E.P.M. I know they are living with the Lord.

While I was finishing this book, on Thursday evening at a prayer meeting we prayed for my sweet little mother asking the Lord to be with her. This was the precise hour when she closed her eyes on her earthly life 1800 miles away. Where two or three are gathered to pray, the Lord will answer your prayers.

My thanks to the pastors who encouraged me to write this book, and to my sister and brother in Christ, Anna S. and Bill D. for sustaining me with encouragement and all around support; to my undaunted editors Frances N. and Candace P., and faithful readers!

I thank the Lord for having blessed me with a wonderful family, Aunt Luise, Uncle Heinrich, Aunt Minna and many friends like Ester, Lotti and Mark, Lisa and Reinhard, Josi O. and Al H., on this side of the ocean and on the other one.

To you and you readers: The Lord let his face shine upon you and give you His peace!
Linthicum, June 4, 1980

I owe my life to Jesus-- You also?

1 Lay no hands upon the family
2 Where is Jesus Christ?
3 I am the Gather's child
4 A Father in Heaven and on earth
5 Christ was born for me
6 What God created is indeed excellent
7 A Sparrow ... but nor forsaken
8 We are created equal
9 Hungry ... you shall be satisfied
10 Leaders have no easy task
11 Store up no treasures
12 Thou shalt not steal
13 I will be with the Lord
14 The Lord's Roses
15 Jesus rules the winds and the sea
16 He preserves our lives
17 Hallowed be Thy name
18 The Lord shall dry your tears
19 I must be in my Father's House
20 ...have a new body and eternal life
21 I know ... I get a home from God
22 You shall be blind for a time
23 Oh heart, take courage!
24 Go feed my sheep!
25 Blessed are they who can hear
26 I am with you in the Spirit
27 The covenant
28 Christ sustains those who abey Him
29 For the Lord none are dispensable
30 Crippling is not necessary
31 He protects and preserves your life
32 I am the Way
33 Fear not, Jesus fights our battles
34 But they who trust in ME shall live
35 The Lord's timing is perfect
36 The Lord is faithful protecting you
37 Be confident, I'll never fail you!
38 by hospitality ..entertained angels
39 Jesus speaks to ordinary people
40 Now don't drop that confidence
41 Set your heart on higher talents
42 Blessed among women are you
43 Teach the very young the love of J.
44 Jesus gave man the power of healing
45 The Lord sticks to his promises
46 What you do to the least of them,
47 Your faith has saved you
48 Never cease to give thanks
49 We too belong to His race
50 Man is sinful by nature
51 I shall lead you to a new country
52 Pray for us too, brothers in Christ
53 Lord why do you pick on me?
54 What rises is immortal
55 Ask, seek, knock and trust you'll
56 Let the dead bury the dead
57 Love is patient and enduring
58 He who has no lave remains in death
59 When Christ appears, you'll be with
60 Your time has not yet come
61 .have been with ME from the beginning
62 Pierced by remorse, confess your love
63 Wherever the Spirit, open freedom
64 The Lord has dealt graciously with us
65 Never grow tired of doing the right!
66 Any realm divided comes to grief
67 God's children in a crooked world
68 Heal the crippled and lame, I ...
69 Faith: teach parents to heal the lame!
70 You names are enrolled in heaven
71 I believe in miracles, yes, I do!
72 ... can be done for one who believes
73 Take courage, you are MINE!

=1010=

1: Lay no hand on the family

JOB 1, 9 - 12:
"There! I leave all she has within your power; but
lay no hand upon the family."

I don't remember my birth. Reflecting on it, I do not
know whether I was loath of entering this world, or
whether the Lord had made a bet with the adversary over
whose child I was to become. At any rate, they fought over
me for four days. I was to have arrived on a Friday, when
my poor mother went into labor ... then on Saturday. Next
I was supposed to be a Sunday child. By the time I arrived
it was Monday at the onset of the bells tolling in the noon
hour, and then only because the doctor pulled me out with
instruments ... ending 56 hours or more of labor. The Lord
had decreed my birth to come on September 24, 1917. My
mother had ordered it to be a boy, but that, too, was up
to the Lord.

2: Where is Jesus Christ?

MATTHEW 18, 10:
   "... For I tell you, their angels in heaven always look upon the face of my father in heaven."

I was in the high-rise pram with large wheels. I hated the confinement. I was "parked" at the foot of five steep steps in front of Bakery Frohberg at the top of a slanted curb.

I had jumped once too often. The pram made itself independent. It tipped backward, the hood opened up by friction and the cushion flopped into the hood. And I? I landed on top of the cushion in the hood. My hands felt the pavement scraping as the pram slid down the slanted sidewalk. I saw three women inside the open shop raise up their hands and cry out:

"Lord Jesus Christ, protect the baby."

I knew that meant me, but I wondered where Jesus Christ was. I was unruffled, rather delighted, because I knew the ground was close enough to contemplate a way out of that prison. However, the women rescued me right away, but I made certain there was no "next time," for I refused to get back into that unreliable vehicle.

Somehow they found a stroller.

3: I am the Father's child

PSALM 46, 2-3, 12:
> "The Lord is our providence and strength, a help in need, therefore we need not fear ... the Lord of Hosts is at our side."

It was wartime throughout my first year of life. My mother and the maid held me to their hearts. They prayed and sighed to the Lord: "Lord be with us ... send us our Father to end the war, have the father return safe and sound ... Yes, Lord, You are alive, the Father liveth and reigneth ... You bring him home to this child safe and sound. Amen!"

We were on the way to the church, the maid and I. She was not really permitted to take me. And when she did, she was supposed to go by bus since the trip was long, very far. The bus was always overcrowded, the ride scary, and the wait for it vexing. For a one-year-old I was a load, but I was good on foot, and Elfriede and I walked. That is, I walked every other block, in order to make "good" time. I never liked to be carried, not really.

I owe my life to Jesus--You also?

Elfriede whiled away the time by telling me stories. As we walked along the city wall, she pointed out a place in the wall:

"A long time ago, when they built this wall, they wanted to build it solid for all times. So they took a baby in a cradle and built the wall over it."

I tried not to look at that part of the wall. "Hoooh", I shivered. I aimed my foot on top of the cobblestone, slid down its far side, straddled the next one and aimed for the middle of the following: "A baby walled up in that city wall to make it solid."

The maid recognized the turmoil in me. We had just gone around the bend through the gap in the wall. She halted under the feeble gas lantern jutting out from the corner of the first house inside the wall. She took my hand tighter into hers. With the other hand she pointed high up, from the base of the church tower into the bleak of the night which had engulfed us, though early afternoon:

"See," she said, "there is the house of God, and from way up there the Father is watching over you and me that nothing evil will ever befall us. **He, the LORD, watches over his children! Fear not, I am your guardian, I am with you to the end of the world.** You, now, trust in Jesus."

I had followed her finger "up there" through the lifeless tree, shrugging my shoulders -- strange place, the abode of the Lord -- the meager glow of the gaslight did not even reach all the way up the tower. The **up there** did not look desirable, but perhaps it was a better place than being walled up in the city wall. The Lord was in the strangest places: in the war ... with me here ... and up there. Even the miserable cobblestones were holy ground. Elfriede had to know, which was comforting and reassuring. We went on.

Elfriede lifted me into her arms: "Look, here we are." She carried me up the four broad steps and opened the great oaken door into the low-ceiling hallway. We entered the parish hall. Everything was lit dimly by two muttering

= 4 =

gas lights. A huge-bellied stove was aglowing red hot.
From it a thick black stovepipe snaked its way through the
room a foot below the ceiling. Women in swaddling black,
wide skirts, ample blouses, scarves and covers, filed in,
filling the backless benches. When we entered the women
made room for Elfriede on a bench against the wall. They
carried huge books thicker than my arm was long. These
they placed on their laps. The door opened and a man with
a long snow-white beard entered. Everyone rose to their
feet and murmered:

"The Lord is a light unto my feet. The Lord let shine
his face upon us and give us peace."

I suppose I went to sleep.

The Lord was also on the bus. When I awakened I knew
I was on the bus. It rumbled, klunked and groaned under
me. I tried to get my bearing, sandwiched amidst a forest
of legs. Under me, at my fingertips, were wooden shoes,
rags, leather shoes. Everything lurched with the bus. It
was Elfriede's voice: "Lord Jesus, watch out for the baby!"
I tried to look up ... skirts and more skirts (it seemed I
had more light below from a bulb marking the steps) ... no
telling whose legs. Someone asked: "Where is the baby?"

"She's alright, sitting on our feet."

The Lord was watching over me ... there was nothing to
fear. I was the Lord's and the Father's child. The next
morning I awakened in my bed.

****

Footnote: "Built into a wall" refers quite literally to Jesus:
Josh. 6, 26; 1 Kings 16, 34; Matthew 21, 42. However
inadvertantly, the knowledge of the maid was quite
supernatural. Folklorists knew what the people said. When I
was about 14 years old, this part of the wall caved in and
archaeologists decided to dig up the foundation. In a
spared out space they did find a baby in a cradle under
the wall. I had never lost the numinous feeling walking
past. Somehow I knew that it was true. My family did not
know about it.

4: A Father in heaven and on earth
JOHN 16, 16-22:

> **"In a little while, you shall behold me no longer; then, after a little, you shall see me ... I go to the Father ... but I shall see you again and your heart will rejoice -- a joy that no one can take from you."**

Nothing was clear to me: "The Father is with you always ... The Father was in the war, the Lord is with the Father ... going to the father, and be returning from the Father, and the father will be returning from the war."

The Lord ended the war, and my father returned from the Somme and Verdun, from mud and cold and deprivation. He was sick. He said:

"The Lord was not in the war. War is an invention of the devil. The church is no good ... pious talk ... they left the fathers dying without comfort, without a shepherd; it was too filthy out there than to risk their lives. What do guns know about human misery! Where was the enemy? Whom did we fight? I have never seen an enemy. I only saw and met frightened, bewildered children of God the Father. Against whom were we ordered to direct the guns? The greedy, who are behind the few who govern, the masterminds of war? They sit in plush-lined chairs by the fire and hope they win the chess-game ... They, the devil's tools...

GOD IS NOT IN WARS!

"The villagers were starved, we were starved ... nobody cared. God sent us a cow ... lost, her stable bombed ... no meadow left, no food ... She mooed piteously. That was the only shot I ordered. She was relieved of her misery, and wandered into our cooking pots, hide and all. The Lord thus helped us and the villagers from starvation."

When my father returned my mother's heart was filled with joy. But my father was often absent. Whenever he came back she again rejoiced ... saddened when he had to leave. The war had made him sick. I, however, knew now that I had a father on earth, and a Father in Heaven; and that the Father in Heaven also was the Father Who guarded over my father in the war ... Who was helping him now to overcome the war, and gain back his health.

5: Christ was born for me

LUKE 2, 9:
> "...and an angel of the Lord flashed upon them, and the glory of the Lord shone all around..."

I don't remember my first Christmas, but my second Christmas is clearly etched into my mind. It was late afternoon or evening. A dim light burned on my mother's night table. I was confined in my mother's king-sized bed ... my mother was resting on it too. The door to my brother's bedroom was locked. Nobody was allowed to go in there. He had not yet arrived. It was very quiet in the house. Nothing stirred. The pendulum of the clock on the wall swung back and forth with a loud tick-tock, and I could hear the beating of my heart.

Suddenly there was a tinkling of many little bells. My mother went slowly to the door and opened it.

Lo and behold, there stood the angel of the Lord in the doorway, and **the glory of the Lord shone all around him.** The angel was clad in white and covered in a cloud of white veil. In his hands he carried a Christmas tree twice his size, sparkling with dozens of burning candles.

Silently the angel walked into the bedroom and placed the tree on the bench before the mirrored wardrobe. He knelt down in prayer, and then turned to go back to the Father in Heaven. Again, the little bells tinkled gaily outside in the hall. The door closed, and the stillness returned.

It was not the same--the room was alive! What magic? There stood the Christmas tree with its heavenly splendor. Angels, animals, pine branches danced over ceiling and walls, multiplied a thousand times by the mirrors. The scent of candles and gingerbread mingled with the dancing stars. A wisp of angel hair was caught in the branches! **Christ was born today,** so that He should know how it feels to be human, with aches and pains and whooping cough, born was hope and love to remain with me forever. **He had come from the Father in Heaven.** The Lord filled my heart with the magic of Christmas to remain with me till today.

6: What God created is indeed excellent

GENESIS 1, 31:

> **"God created the world, and everything therein ... and so it was. God saw all that he had made, and found it indeed excellent."**

My brother was born. My father was back at home, but now my mother stayed in the hospital with my brother. Elfriede and I walked once a day through the park to the hospital to wave to my mother, but most of the time the window remained closed. Yet there in the park was a peacock preserve with peacocks strutting up and down, or engrossed in palaver. Well apart from the peacocks were three ponds ... one for skating, one for ice cutting and one for the swans. Snow covered the ground. The swans owned a residence at the edge of one pond. One time the game warden let me take a peek inside the swan house. There was a large soft nest in which, covered by down, feathers and straw, was one very large egg. Another week and no one was allowed near the little house, for the swan guarded it at all times and let no one near. From then on only one swan was out fishing for worms and grubs in the open pond. The swans were expecting babies.

My mother and brother remained in the hospital, so my grandmother came and took me along to grandfather's. They lived in an ancient house. The guestroom was built over the thoroughfare to the street. It provided a perfect shelter for the swallows, where they had built their nests. From dawn until sunset the swallows swished in and out. The guestroom was occupied by the occupational forces that is, a Frenchman was living there. I could not understand his speech and he could not understand mine, a little puzzling, but we hit it off well. I had been watching the swallows from below, he called me up, and now he showed me what they were up to. From his window we could see into their nests below.

There in one nest lay five green, or bluish speckled eggs. And while we were looking one of them developed a black hole, so did a second one. Soon we were looking into the yellow-lined mouth of a hungry baby swallow. The mother and father returned with a flurry of wings. Each carried a worm. This was swallowed, then dropped into their baby's mouth. Before long they had two to feed. They took turns in feeding them standing on the rim of the nest. From below the cat watched them flying to and fro. God had fixed it that the cat could not reach the nest. The babies thrived and grew bigger every day. There were five to feed. Before long they filled the whole nest, their mouths always open.

Then one day there was great commotion. Flying, like walking, had to be learned. Swallow parents teamed together. Three old swallows covered the cat in the courtyard. The others began to talk to the babies. A pigeon baby, round and plump, also was chased out of the nest, evidently for flying lessons ... the pigeon parents were frantic. They, too, wished the protection of the swallows over the cat. The swallows pushed the little ones out of the nest. The babies fluttered to the nearest bush below. The parents alighted a little higher on the same twig and moved toward the tip, the little one moved until the tip gave way, air-born the baby flew back to the nest. Rested, the parent pushed it out again, starting all over.

The pigeon's parents, with their only one, had a frightful time. They had it cornered on the ledge. Finally it simply plummeted right in front of the cat. The three swallows saw it happen. Before the surprised pussy could stretch out her claws, they swooped upon her and threatened to peck out her eyes. The cat yelped as it jumped to safety disappearing inside the house. God had protected the pigeon baby. But the day was not long enough for the pigeon's parents to coax and coo their baby back up to the nest. Finally grandfather put up a chicken ladder. The baby pigeon fluttered from one level to the other until it was safe at home.

Grandfather also helped the honey bees. He fed them through the winter, and built new houses for them, each a different color. He brought a new house to them when they swarmed. The bees knew how to make honey, and honey meant shoes, clothes and candle wax. The Lord had thought of everything.

7: A Sparrow ... but not forsaken

PSALM 25, 16-17:
> **"Turn to me and have pity, for I am lonely and low;
> relieve the anguish of my heart..."**

The swallows had moved south, and a cold wind blew, I do not know whence. As I have explained, the devil must have made a pact with the Lord long before I was born. Before I was six I had experienced what it means to have lived the happiest childhood a heart could desire and a half of a lifetime, which had a taste of hell. The second half began shortly after my third birthday.

My mother and my brother had made it home from the hospital safely. I returned to my hometown without my grandfather or grandmother, negotiating the trip on the train alone, yet I knew the Lord was with me. My father and mother, both, were at the railroad station to welcome me. They were healthy and anxious, perhaps a little weak. I was a sturdy three-year-old. The sun had set and darkness fell. I did not recognize them.

"My mother lives in the hospital, and my father is in the hospital, and a brother I have also living in the hospital."

I owe my life to Jesus--You also?

That was the opening clue for my mother: "Yes, you have a brother. Let's leave the railroad station and see for yourself."

I agreed under the circumstances. There was also no alternative. Two miles is a long way for a three-year-old at the end of a busy day. In retrospect, I wonder why no transportation was arranged, for the walk must have been taxing for my mother, and perhaps even for my father. By midway I had reached a crisis. The walk was a marathon. I crumbled and said:

"The child wants to be carried."

My father replied: "Up, the child is to march."

I was shocked at the sound of his voice. I got up to my feet. I was pulled on the right arm and the left. The tempo was accelerated; I could not fall. Only when we turned into Elizabeth Street did I know where I was, and what they had said was true. This truly was my home, but the luster had gone out of my life. I ached all over, with no reserves left.

My parents lifted me up to see my brother. "What do you say now?" They looked at me expectantly.

What was I to say? The size of him ... I had played with others' brothers, rough and tough. This brother was a mere doll, and could not compare. My parents waited anxiously, so I said the only thing that came to mind:

"Wouldn't you do better to take him back to the hospital and trade him in for a sister?"

Food was set before me with a command to eat. I would not. Gruffly, I was cleaned from the trip and dumped to bed. I was grateful for my bed. I was not forsaken, I knew the Lord's eyes were watching over me.

Matthew 10, 29:

"Are not two sparrows hardly worth a nickel? Yet not one of them will fall to the ground unless your Father wills it."

8: We are created equal

1 JOHN, 1-3:
"My beloved, we are all God's children ...
That we are equal before the Lord."

My little brother was sick. The maid was busy. My mother was occupied with the baby. I was allowed to watch the bathing. Of course, I noticed the anatomical difference, and asked what it was. My next question was whether I had that, too, when I was **that** little. The maid and my mother laughed and said "yes". I wanted to know what had happened to it. "Oh, that just disappeared inside," they said.

Very well, I had no further questions. All things were created equal before God. That boys and girls could not be equal never entered my mind. That, however, this scrap of brother should be on a par with myself, I was not about to buy. He would mind no one and could do nothing but scream, even though he was not supposed to. I was convinced that the anatomical difference, too, would equalize, but it mattered very little that it did not.

I was equal, and my father considered me worthy of lessons in leadership. I was lonely, and I suppose he was lonely too. His presence was no more wanted in the room with my mother and my brother than was mine. The baby was sick, and the Father in heaven was especially beseeched at night when no one in the house could sleep. My father taught me that leadership brought about responsibility for all those who depend on their decisions. If one suffers, all would suffer. When they hurt Jesus, his disciples and those who loved him had to suffer too. And my father added: "As long as we are living we are to do our best, to love and help each other."

9: Hungry ... you shall be satisfied

LUKE 6, 20-21, 38:
**"Blessed are you poor! The realm of God is yours.
Blessed are you who hunger today! You shall be
satisfied ... Give, and you will have ample measure
given you--"**

The times between 1920 and 1924 were very hard. Nearly
two thirds of all the families I knew did not have enough to
eat. My father had many friends. He was a war hero ...
that is, he saved the lives of many while in the war, and
now they came from near and far, bringing milk, butter,
vegetables, potatoes, soup from butchering, meat, or
whatever they could spare. It did not mean we could open a
store, but we did have enough. And the Lieutenant, that is
what they all called my father, was very frugal as always,
and shared the surplus with old pensioners who would have
starved long before had it not been for his weekly rounds.
Since my mother did not want me to disturb my brother, I
accompanied my father. He knew the whole town, and the
whole town knew me.
My father was a teacher and he kept on telling me about
leadership. One time he complained about the children being
naughty instead of doing something constructive. I asked:
"What do you mean by that?"...
He answered: "Well, there are many things they could do
instead of wasting their time and hurting others. They can
help those women who have lost fathers in the war, such as
bringing wood into the kitchen, running errands, carrying
coal supplies, helping in the garden, picking potatoes in
the field, gleaning wheat fields ..." There was no end to
his suggestions.

When I first started, I was three and a half years old.
Winter was on the way out. One of the older boys was
caught at thievery, and was paddled severely. His crime:
he could no longer look on as his brothers and sisters
starved, so he would steal a loaf of bread, and this time
was caught. I never asked him any questions, but knew he
was hungry. He had no place to go, and I had none to go

to either. I asked him if he would like to play with me and earn gold stars in heaven (that was what I had learned in Sunday School), but I added, "I am only allowed to play with children who go to Sunday School. Can you promise me to be in Sunday School next Sunday?"

I had not expected anything less, he had promised it, and he lived up to his promise. This was the beginning of my "gang". We'd meet after school six days a week, after 1 P.M. The other children, admitted after equally soul searching questions, were in the same predicament as he. I do not know what my mother, or the maid, thought about my appetite, but I never left the kitchen without loaded pockets. But I also made sure that wrappers were treated very gently and, when empty, folded neatly and returned to my pockets (paper was a rare commodity, even news print!). As I told you, I knew the town, and I always had a way of finding out from my father who needed help ... and people were used to seeing me.

At first we were five, very soon seven, and then eleven, ranging up to 11 years old. We went to an old crippled lady, Mrs. Kister. She and Mr. Kister took care of four little grandchildren. She needed help but could not afford it. There was a lot of work to be done -- carry water, split wood, peel potatoes, hoe the garden, feed the chickens, guard the children. Ursula, the oldest, every so often fell down with cramps. I walked into her kitchen and asked, "How many can you feed with extra soup for doing your chores?"

She sized up the gang, then she said, "Two for two meals a day, and three more for one meal each week."

That was deemed very generous. Truly, the kids made the woman very glad and often by three o'clock she had everything ship-shape. Meanwhile, I commanded the children out of underfoot to the meadow. As a veteran of two years in kindergarten, I taught them games and dances to songs. This way none of the little ones would hamper the workers. That job done, we would ball-play ourselves into position for the next job. I was the only one who owned a ball, but it was out of my hands, they loved it.

Dr. Bliesnick needed the gang to pick cherries. I kept after the baker until he finally accepted my first member for the job of distributing rolls to the wealthy before school

I owe my life to Jesus-- You also?

early in the morning. His wages: all the bread his family needed, which was literally worth millions then, because he had eight brothers and sisters.

We helped certain washer-women spread out the wet laundry to bleach on the grass and keep the geese from walking over the drying pieces.

To collect the promised meals the boys and girls brought along a motley array of kettles. None was ever disappointed, and the better they did the chores, the heavier the kettles were to take home for their families. When one source dried up, I found a better replacement. After all, soon my gang was experienced. Several times we played ourselves some four miles into the woods to the hut of a charcoal burner. He had broken a leg and his two children were too little to handle his affairs. My 11 could do it. But before he was willing we had a time. First he had to explain to me why we could not do it, and what it entailed. The older children huddled and figured out the best for each job. Then they showed him that they could do it well. For a number of weeks the older ones worked very hard, they even pulled his products to the market in a four-wheeled handwagon, returning with his groceries. I think he hired two permanently.

On Sunday mornings I started out for church shortly after 9 A.M. I stopped in front of various houses on the way. I picked up the Kister children and was met by the others. The charcoal burner's children met me at church. I was a pied piper with a regular following of over 20 children, and "my" class had to be divided at least 5 times into more sections. Jesus Christ made them all very good children and none of them was beaten up again. They were poor, but they had willing hands offering help where needed, and in turn their needs were stilled.

Praise the Lord! Hallelujah!

10: Leaders have no easy task

GENESIS 3, 19: "... In the sweat of your brow you shall earn your food ..."

When fall came I generously hired out the whole gang to help pick potatoes from two fields. Schools were closed for potato recess. Praise the Lord, this did not include my private kindergarten. But come 1 P.M. I was also committed to show up. From 1 P.M. until 6 P.M. I followed row upon row retrieving potatoes from the lightly plowed soil, and throwing them into baskets spaced at regular intervals. Leaders, if they are worth their salt, have no easy life, to quote my father, and I could not set a poor example. I worked as fast as the others ... my back ached. How about the others? They had been at it since 7 in the morning.

When the fields were finished, the farmer and his wife were relieved and pleased. He asked my gang to line up for a count. There were forty-five in all, which included brothers and sisters as well as friends. He asked for the leader. He looked down at the scrap of me, and asked:

"What are the wages, young Miss?"

I knew from my father that the harvest was very good. "Sir," I said, "you had agreed to pay one bag of potatoes for each family ... this makes five bags (several hundred pounds each)." And I held up five fingers for emphasis.

The farmer hesitated ... probably a stiff bargain, worth millions. I shrugged my shoulders, and explained, "A number of us ... such as I ... don't want anything. It is only for the ones who truly need it."

"Alright, line up by families; the others even out the

lines, the farmer said and huddled with his wife debating. They decided to pay the wages. He emptied baskets to create five piles.

I ordered: "Count all the potatoes in each heap so that it is fair and equal!"

There were no sacks. Guards were posted, the rest filled their aprons and ran home to solicit help to carry home their potatoes. It had turned dark.

I came home late for supper and got a beating for being late, then a second one for looking filthy, and a third for not coming home when called. Well, the dear Lord knew I had been busy! No one asked me for an explanation, and had they listened, they wouldn't have believed me. The Lord had made me feel really happy about the successful day. Nothing else really mattered. The next morning I was as stiff as an old grandmother ... probably from the beating. At least I got some sympathy from the maid, who rubbed my poor back with liniment.

Come 1 P.M. I met my gang. I told them what had happened to me. None of them laughed ... they all were sore. We decided to call it a day. We sat in our favorite spot in the sunshine singing songs and telling stories. Some of the older children fell sound asleep ... that, too, was alright. When the sun went down, and the bell from the tower announced the fifth hour, I gave the signal: playing tag they raced me home.

LUKE 12,48:
"He who has much given him will have much required from him, and he who has much entrusted to him will have all the more demanded of him."

11: Store up no treasures

MATTHEW 6, 19-21:
**"Store up no treasures for yourselves on earth ...
where thieves steal ... for where your treasure lies,
your heart will lie there too."**

My little brother's life eventually was established. My
mother waited over his very breath day and night. He was
not to cry, not under any circumstances, or he could
rupture. May He who has wisdom understand it. I could be
made to scream with pain, and no one would worry that I
could rupture. My troubles increased with inclement
weather, or when it was inconvenient to let me out of the
house. Then I was to be "my brother's keeper."

By the time he was two years of age my brother could
get around on two feet. He did not have to talk to get
things ... I don't believe he could talk by then. He had a
lot of toys ... in fact, he did not know what to do with
them all. I had my own toys, or so I thought. We shared
the same room, and there was really no place where I could
hide anything from his eyes. Those toys that were lying

around unused were of no interest to him. But let anything
be moving, it would catch his fancy as it would that of a
kitten, only, he was as mobile as a bag of molasses. It did
not matter what it was. Sometimes he'd sit on toys, with
toys in his lap and both hands full, and yet he'd open his
ugly mouth, close his eyes and scream bloody murder.

I knew a bamboo stick was behind the door. Fear and
panic welled up in me. I took his head and pointed him in
the direction where the object of his latest desire lay
abandoned. Too late, my mother already had heard his
screams. She flew into the room, and saw him scream as if
desperate. She grabbed me in one hand and the bamboo
stick in the other. She worked me with all her might from
head to toe, shouting:

"You are not to murder that little boy, he is your
brother, I will teach you respect for life ... this is how it
feels when one is murdered." She would not let up until
she had spent her strength, and the stick had no feelings
... it whistled in her hand.

After that, my heart laid no more claims on anything. A
whimper and Jerry had what he wanted. He knew his power
over me, and with the years developed schemes by which to
nurture his mother's solicitude. After that I called nothing
mine. The Lord knew it, for He, too, was beaten and
despised, and betrayed. Jesus was not liked in his
hometown, only he had no place to lay his head. I was
richer than he, for I had food and drink, a warm bed and
lots of friends on the outside. I knew Jesus was with me
... He grieved with me. For the Lord knew how it feels,
because He had felt grief when the people did it to Him.
Jesus was not able to fight the system, and neither could
I. Jesus comforted me, being mother and father to me. He
sustained me in his love.

12: I know when you steal

THE COMMANDMENT: "Thou shalt not steal."

I had no trouble getting up early. Day in, day out, the maid would start the fires in the stove, then help me to dress, so in turn I could help the maid. My family liked to sleep late. I usually had my breakfast in the kitchen. Sundays, I was permitted to leave early to pick up the other children for Sunday School. When I was three and one half years old we moved to a large house on Possen Drive, lined with huge chestnut trees. This was closer to the church and I established a new route picking up my friends, doubling our class.

We also had a fruit cellar where my father and mother placed carefully-picked apples and pears on racks. At the time the country was raked by inflation. One loaf of bread cost a million. I watched older children fill their slates with zeros to add up just the expenses for one day. There were not enough millions in circulation to buy their daily needs, and many had to go to sleep on empty stomachs. People were desperate, and thievery was rampant. Our fruit cellar had to be locked at all times.

One bright and sunny day we were playing hide and seek and I hid in the cellar. I found the fruit cellar open. The pears smelled delicious, and I stretched out my hand for the biggest one. Then a voice said softly but firmly:
"THOU SHALT NOT STEAL"

I was shocked. Though I put the fruit back, I said out loud: "But no one will know that I took it!"

And the voice came back to me just a bit closer and louder: **"YES, BUT I KNOW IT!"**

"But, where are you?"

"I AM WITH YOU ALWAYS!"

I looked everywhere, incredulous I let my eyes followed the light through the cellar window into the blue, blue sky.

I had had enough of the cellar. I tiptoed out of that holy place and closed the metal door the way I had found it. I went upstairs and reported to my mother that the door was unlocked. She would not believe me, and she dared me. She finally made me go with her. It was, as I had said, unlocked. She locked it. She did not believe me that I had not taken a fruit, so I did not get one for supper.

Jesus Christ knew the truth. Why did I have to be punished? Somehow I did not mind the punishment. I had not been so virtuous about the fruit, and after all, it was something special to have a secret with the Lord.

The next day, my father took my hand and led me into the cellar, holding the key to the fruit cellar. He opened the door and asked me seriously:

"Did you truly not take a fruit yesterday?"

I told him how I was hiding and found it open.

"Did you not eat a pear?"

I said **"NO"** with emphasis.

"Alright, I believe you. Now pick what you want, one for the right hand and one for the left, and disappear ... don't betray me to mother."

I was as happy as a lark: now I had secrets with two fathers. I picked the pear from the day before; the other really did not matter. I started munching while watching my father carefully fill the two gaps in the front row. No pears have ever tasted **sooo** delicious!

13: I will be with the Lord

LUKE 20, 38:

> "GOD is not a GOD of dead people, but of the living ... I will be with the FATHER ..."

Chimney-sweeps bring good luck. When a chimney-sweep shows himself all the children gather in the street and try to touch him, and then themselves. The little black marks they carried happily as a sign that they had touched luck. Today the chimney-sweep rode his bike right up to our house door and disappeared inside with all his paraphernalia. He asked to be led into the attic. There he pushed a ladder to the steep roof, swung himself on top to the chimney and began to sweep. The maid, my mother, everyone ran from room to room shutting the flues and close the stoves to confine the soot to the chimney.

Beneath us lived Pastor Steinhof and Minna, his housekeeper. Pastor Steinhof was a wonderful old gentleman who loved to read stories to me. He had been a missionary. Now he was confined to a chair. He was very, very old, perhaps 100 years. His feet failed him. He had a beard a yard long and snowy white; around his pate he had sort of a halo of white long hair. His feet were bundled into a large checkered blanket. On the right side always stood a little table piled with his books and to the left stood the stove. I heard him call just as the chimney-sweep received his pay and cluttered down the stairs.

Dear Pastor Steinhof! Nobody had closed his flue, or closed the doors of the stove. Now all the "luck" a chimney-sweep could bring had settled over him. His beard was black, and black was his hair, so were his nose, face and hands. His housekeeper had gone shopping. He was a sight to behold, and he exclaimed:
"Don't touch anything in the room!"

It was a disaster. I ran into the returning housekeeper. I alarmed my mother. Women folk streamed hither. There he sat as black as could be, comforting the dumbstruck folk. They sprung to life. All combined forces. They bathed the old gentleman and put him into a rocking chair out on the lawn. They let everything from his room follow him into the sunshine. Rugs, drapes, books ... everything had to be cleaned, including the walls. By the time the sun set everything was back in its usual place, and Pastor Steinhof sat once more in his chair by the stove, asking the Lord's blessings upon the women who had worked so hard to repair the damage.

When winter came around I stopped in on him at the usual hour. He made me sit down on my little foot stool and listen very carefully. He said: "Hilla, remember me. In a little while I will die and be buried. But that isn't really true. You will see it by my smile, that I am only sleeping. This is because the Lord will come and pick me up and take me to His heavenly home, a beautiful place, where I can walk again. I am looking forward to this last trip, meeting our Lord and staying with Him forever. Now, don't let anyone know our secret, keep it for yourself. I am all excited to meet the Lord."

He closed his eyes. His face shone with radiance. He was very, very quiet. I tiptoed out of the room, closing the door gently behind me. He never heard me leave. He was with the Lord.

Next morning, when I came downstairs all the doors to his apartment stood wide open. My mother was weeping, as were all the others. I climbed on a chair to see. There he was, lying on his bed, his hands folded over the Bible, from which he had read to me. I said shyly: "Don't weep ... see his smile, he is on his last trip, he's been picked up by the Lord."

I was whisked out of the room ... "This is no place for children."

14: The Lord's Roses

1 PETER 1, 23-24:
   "...Its flower fades, but the LORD's word lasts for ever..."

I had another friend ... he nurtured a rose garden. He talked to the roses, like the Frenchman to the swallows. He kept them free of bugs, watered them, trimmed them, mulched them and, when the time came, bundled them up against the winter. I think he must not have liked children, or perhaps, children did not like roses. I loved to watch him by the hour, especially early in the morning before kindergarten. At first I squatted on the wall outside the iron picket fence. Then I was permitted to sit inside the fence. Gradually I was allowed to help with the weeding, and then learned all about roses.

"When you are in the LORD'S BUSINESS, you are responsible for his creation ... the roses don't worry about the morrow. But to bloom their best they require lots of love and care," the aged explained.

I owe my life to Jesus--You also?

His roses showed his care. They won prizes at exhibitions. He let me smell the different aromas. No two smelled alike. Once a week, he asked me which rose I would like to have. And each time I knew I hurt him by asking for his most favorite one. Each time he touched his heart, looked lovingly at the prize, smelled it, hesitated, and then cut it just at the right length. He carefully handed it to me and watched me leave for home. There my treasure was deposited into one of my mother's favorite vases.

The old man and I were friends. But then a day came when he missed coming into his rose garden, and his roses missed him, too. I went and watered the roses just right. I weeded them, and I found the snippers to clip off the wilted blossoms just as he used to do. When he returned, he found everything in astounding order. He said the Lord had helped him. I laughed. Then he was serious. He said:

"The Lord has given each of us talents, and it is our duty to make the most of them. Some have the gift to talk to the flowers ... they are part of the wonders of God's creation. He gives the roses and us our temperament, our clothing, our food and needs. He has created everything so perfectly, so that we, his children, can rejoice in their beauty."

Then he added: "I am old, sick and weary ... every day I will be in the garden for a shorter period. When winter comes I will go to the Lord to tender the roses in heaven."

I made my daily trips even after the roses were wrapped up by a professional gardener. He spent his last weeks on a lounge chair in the winter garden. Then they would not let me in any longer.

Then one bleak day a black coach stopped in front of our house to pick me up. Two Swedish children, a little older than I, were inside. They handed me a basket with rose petals ... I knew now that he had gone to tend the Lord's rose garden. He had asked for my presence at his funeral. Together with his grandchildren I was to strew his last earthly way with rose petals.

The organ played a requiem (from Brahms) and some one sang: "They go away aweeping, bearing precious seeds ... all life, it is like the roses, when the wind blows wintery, they wither and die ... but in heaven our Lord and Father is waiting, beautiful rooms are readied ... death, where is your power? ... the Lord reigneth forever."

The singing still lingered. We three walked before the closed coffin. I knew he could smell the fragrant petals that ran through my fingers. He had planned it that way. The last petals left in the basket ... I sent them ahead into the open grave. The coffin was lowered, and the straps removed. Then I was given a shovel to throw a handful of earth on top of the coffin.
"Earth to earth, life to life" ... I had lost a dear friend.

Spring brought new flowers, but the roses were gone, perhaps moved to Sweden. That was good, for it would not have been the same. But I asked for a flower bed of my own. I got it. It, too, had to have a rose bush, but somehow it did not really matter. I soon found that I could achieve amazing results by adding all the varieties of flowers I could lay my hands on to this cramped bit of ground. By the time I was 7, I had to discover that the Lord had too many varieties to be represented in my garden patch. Nevertheless, from snow drops in earliest spring to chrysanthemums at the onset of winter, I had something blooming. I was generous in making early visits with flowers in my hand. Giving flowers was fun. My mother loved them, tiny or large. I loved to grow them and give them away. Cut flowers ... Lord teach me, that my life must have an end soon, and that I must part from here ... the flower petals ran through my fingers ... they still smell faintly of HIS roses . . .

I owe my life to Jesus--You also?

15: Jesus rules the winds and the sea

MATTHEW 8, 24-26:
Now a heavy storm came on at the lake, so that the boat was buried under the waves ... "Help, LORD, we are drowning!" Then HE got up and checked the winds and the sea, and there was a great calm.

I was five years old when I learned to swim. My father and I met, each in his loneliness. My mother was preoccupied with my brother who was not well. God's world held peace, and my father liked long walks with the Lord. He walked me to fresh springs, and taught me to build water mills in a valley called "the Brueckental". He showed me how the Lord preserved wind roses and snow drops underneath the snow. We inspected the fields with winter wheat. When summer came, his students slated him to be judge at a swim meet. I was welcome to tag along; all had pledged to keep an eye on me.

They dived and they swam. My father was briefed as to his duties, and I listened and absorbed everything. As the meet dragged on, I decided to try my hand at it. I dived in and swam ... it worked for me, too!

That was not the intent of the meet. "Man over board!" the whistles blew. A guard nearest to the bridge, in an elegant white suit, was at my side in a sleek dive. He led me back to the bridge, where my father sat and assured him that no harm had come to me. I took up my seat again at his feet on the planks. My seat had hardly dried when I moved again closer to the edge about two yards above the water. Fanfares announced high dives. And I? I did just that. Again the show was stopped by shrill whistles. Again the guard fished me back out to the grass. But this time he did not take the trouble to apologize to my father, and I saved him the trip back to the bridge. I meekly went there to take up my old seat again. Then they played an exhibition water ball game. They turned right, and they turned left. What fun! I could do that too! And while everyone was intent on the game, I was right in the middle ... My activity interfered with the order of the day.

Awards were given out, and my father was about to take his seat after his speech when the chairman of the meet detained him. Before the assembly of the crowd the chairman thanked my father for his competent participation as a non-swimmer (applause). Then he said: "I am sentencing you, Dr. Lotz, to bring your daughter, pointing at me, twice each week for swimming lessons (lots of applause). The instructions will be free as a contribution by the association." Laughter and more applause! ... Lucky for me, they really meant it. By the end of the season I swam like a fish.

That winter my brother had pneumonia (I was in the first grade) and could not recover. The doctor recommended a climate change. By April I received dispensation from school, and my mother, brother and I boarded the train for Velden on the Woerter Lake in Austria.

When we arrived it rained and rained and would not stop. The lake was enshrouded in a cloud, then one thunderstorm after another roared through the valley. They called it "Foehn Wind." I watched the Lord's fireworks from the safety of the window. I saw the wind descend a mountain slope and plow a street through the woods with a mighty roar. The lake looked cold and forbidding. It had spilled over its banks by some 50 feet or so. The angry waters had completely hidden the swimming pool; and the small-craft marina, usually high and dry, had its tower barely sticking out of the water.

But then, at long last, came the day with blue sky and no wind. The birds sang love songs and the sky bathed in the lake without a ripple. Boats appeared from everywhere, and my mother also took out a boat, plying the oars. This was only for swimmers ... my brother had to stay on shore. I leaned over and trailed a hand in the water. I lost track of time. Suddenly, as I gazed into the water, the face of the sky had changed to an ugly darkness. As I straightened out the sea began to heave the boat. My mother's oar swung useless into the air.

A white motorboat streaked through the angry waves bearing down on us. Someone jumped into our boat, grabbed me and tossed me into waiting arms. Then they lifted my mother into the launch, fastened our boat behind while the skipper pointed again into the mountainous waves. He steered for the next row boat, two, three, four and more until the capacity was dangerously exceeded. They had a wireless radio device on board, and the skipper checked with Velden ... no chance for a safe landing there. He set the course for Poertschach. People anchored themselves under the benches, doused periodically with water. I had found a space under the skipper's bench. I could not slip out from under, being held by dowels on all six sides including up and down, and no one else could fit into that space. I could hear the skipper's orders and understand the wind-swept answers, or guess them. They picked up two more boats. Our boat was overloaded and the little boats became a liability, threatening to be crashed against our boat. One by one they were turned over to the sea. The ropes were used to tie the men to the boat. We were dashing into the mountainous waves, which threatened to swallow us, boat and all. A window shattered.

Off and on in the dark we saw the pilot light from Poertschach. Our boat swung into a hole in the lake, and way above us loomed the landing bridge like a giant scaffold. The men on the ropes were lined up on the opposite side, two of them holding a woman between them. Like a giant elevator the motorboat was lifted up, the skipper turned the wheel toward the open lake -- the waves swung it to complete the turn and we sidled up to the top of the pier. The men hurled the women unto stretched tarpaulins on the bridge. And down we swirled into an

I owe my life to Jesus--You also?

abyss clear of the pier. This maneuver was repeated time and again. Now the boat was light enough to venture into shallower water to a more sheltered place on the pier. I saw my mother make it. Then the captain shouted, "You, down there, out, you are next!"

I untangled myself from the prison of bars into sturdy arms, and the man jumped with me on top of the pier. The lake nearly followed us. When the spray cleared, the boat was swallowed up. I was worried about the captain, but the man said, "Don't worry about him, he is in the Lord's hands, they know the lake, the winds and the waves. Before long, you will see him with us."

He had run with me into the hotel, the angry spray following us. Now he set me back on my feet. Towels and blankets! What a solicitude, but we needed it. Now that we were safe we looked blue and shivered like leaves in a soft breeze.

Then the door opened with an icy blast. I let out a shout of joy: IT WAS OUR PILOT! With him were a dozen of men from Poertschach. He had succeeded on first try to put his boat into the automatic slip and they had hoisted it free of the angry waves. The engine shut itself off: it had run out of gasoline!

Just in time ... now the storm truly unleashed. It threatened the whole waterfront and the hotel itself. The fires were put out. The wooden shutters kept us from looking out. The lake jumped on top of the roof. Huddled in blankets as we were, we all knelt and prayed to the Lord to stop the wind and calm the water. Jesus Christ listened to us and suddenly the wind stopped blowing. Someone opened the doors, and then the shutters. Black clouds opened up, pouring down a deluge. Then the rain fizzled out. The sun bored a hole into the clouds, at first just one beam, then a whole bundle. Soon there were rainbows all over the lake. The waves dissipated. By the time I had a hot glass of chocolate we once more had bright daylight. It was five hours later, just 3 o'clock in the afternoon.

I owe my life to Jesus--You also?

"By train, or by boat?" the skipper asked.

"By boat, with you!" I shouted.

It was decided, and my mother didn't have much choice (also, she had no money with her in the boat). The motor boat was launched into the water with us, with a safe number of people on board. Off we went out into the calm sea. We located four wooden boats on our course, all upside down. The men strung them up behind us with their white bottoms glistening in the sunshine. We picked up stray oars.

Our boat-house, usually high and dry on land, sat now practically on top of the water. There was not enough clearance. We had to take on more ballast. Every one had to stay on board. When the waves receded, the skipper breathed hard. He gave a blast to the engine and shut it off. The boat was caught on the tracks inside and hoisted free of the water. The boat was safe and we were on dry land once more.

A huge crowd had watched the maneuver, and now took charge of us all. Our skipper got a hero's welcome, and so did we. They carried us in triumph back to Hotel Moeslacher. A priest came and gave thanks for the miraculous rescue ... even men wept. Everyone had, however, enough for the day, and by 7 P.M. nothing in the hotel stirred. All the warm bottles and hot bricks had been put into operation, creating warm nests for the cold and weary seafarers. The Lord had been with us all the way.

"and he who does not risk his life for others shall lose his life -- and he who gives his life for others shall gain new life."

Without Christ Jesus, our skipper would not have succeeded.

16: HE preserves our lives

JOHN 10, 12-17:
" ...The hired man, who is not the shepherd and does not own the sheep, deserts them when he sees danger coming; he runs away ... This is why my father loves me, because I lay down my life to take it up again ..."

The lake was flooded. But the sun gained more and more power, and the lake began to recede. The boats were able to get out again. The deck of the swimming pool appeared clear from the water. Once the railing was fully exposed, I was permitted to take up swimming again. The huge L-shaped deck was slanting toward the water. It was slick ... every board a slide of 20 yards or more. The lake was deep ... they said, beyond the edge of the deck some 400 feet. That was 100 times my size. It did not matter to me for I could swim. I had company ... others were also taking dips. Deep waters are cold waters ... the temperature hardly reached 60 degrees ... yet swimming was far preferable to guarding my brother.

The swimming pool was no place for my little brother, but once in a while my mother would come along with him and bathe in the warm sunshine on toweling on the deck. So it was one lovely day. I had been in the water, my brother in the sun. My mother had changed his clothing, and I was fully dressed too. Now all the adults disappeared into the cabins to change for dinner. My brother and I were to wait for my mother. My brother ran on the newly exposed part of the deck, the beginning of a 20-foot slide, faster and faster ... he didn't even have time to scream. He shot underneath the open railing right into the deepest deep.

I dashed after him by the same route. Before I dived in head-first, I saw both his hands above his head below the murky water. I grabbed one hand and swam toward the ladder. Two rungs were above water, round wood and slimy. What to do? There was not a wiggle out of my brother, which probably was my salvation. I yanked him up, slipped his arms and head over the upper rung and held his heels between my knees on the lower one, his stomach came to rest on the upper one. The rough treatment squeezed the water out of his lungs. It ran out of his nose, mouth and ears ... anyway. Now, that I had regained my breath and could have shouted for help, I was spared that task. My brother had rallied. He began to scream bloody murder, with no place to go. He was perfectly normal, as far as I was concerned. And his yelling? For once, I did not mind it.

It seemed to take an eternity, spent partly in the cold water. My brother's cries went under the deck farthest from the cabins. I could hear foot-fall, and faint shouts. It was clear, we were missed; they were searching ... people looking everywhere. Finally they heard the screams. Two men came dashing our way. They slipped too and fell fully dressed into the lake. One grabbed me and the other my brother, they lifted us up to the railing. They could not make that ladder either and had to swim around to the other one.

I was scolded for having pushed my brother down the slippery way, and for being wet in my Sunday dress. My mother bundled up my brother in the towels and carried him home. A nice couple invited me up into their sun-bath tower. I stripped, and we hung my clothes all over the railing to dry. I went to sleep between them, surrounded by God's sun and love. I had done my part ... there was no doubt in my soul. Now I knew my mother was happy with my brother safe and sound.

17: Hallowed be Thy name

MATTHEW 6, 8-13:
> **Your father knows your needs before you ask him.**
> **Let this be how you pray:**

"OUR FATHER IN HEAVEN . . ."

The summer was spent. The vacationers were leaving Hotel Moeslacher in Velden at the Woerter Lake. We left, too. I had been graduated in absentia from the first grade to the second grade, and I was in for a surprise. Before I had left, it had been mandatory to write in Gothic script ... when I returned Latin script was required. Also, my class had learned to recite long poems; I knew none of them. The teacher was benign:

"You do not have to make up any of those, except this

I owe my life to Jesus--You also?

one. Take it home with you."

I met my father at the garden gate. He wanted to know:
"How did everything go?"
"Oh, rough. I have to write now in Latin script."
"That is alright, don't you want to be able to read my
letters? What else?"
"I have to learn a long poem."
"What is it about?"
"Well, I have not read it, but ... well, it is about,
about **the father**."
His laughter bounded off the house and was swallowed
by the leaves of the chestnut trees: "Perhaps you can get
out of that one also. Let me see!" I handed him the folded
paper, and he read out loud with his trained formal voice:

**"Our Father, Who art in heaven; Hallowed be Thy Name;
Thy kingdom come; Thy will be done on earth, as it is in
heaven; Give us this day our daily bread; And forgive us
our trespasses, as we forgive those who trespass against
us; And lead us not into temptation; But deliver us from
evil; For Thine is the kingdom, and the power, and the
glory, for ever and ever. Amen."**
His eyes twinkled: "You learn that, it might come in
handy one of these days. Let's copy that 10 times in Latin
script ... you can do that job sitting at my desk, so that
mother and brother will not bother you."

So I sat under the supervision of two fathers, safe from
tribulations. Little of my writing turned out beautiful, much
of it was mediocre, but very little unreadable. As it turned
out, I had long known the Lord's Prayer by heart from
Sunday School and ... :

"LORD FORGIVE ME, AS I FORGIVE THEM."

18: The Lord shall dry your tears

REVELATION 7, 17:
"...For the lamb ... will be their shepherd, guiding them to fountains of living water; and GOD shall wipe every tear from their eyes."

My troubles were many, and now I was literally green. It was merciful that I could not stay at home. My mother and my brother had been in the hospital, and now they were afraid of infection. I had been with Aunt Kuhlmann when I took sick. They blamed cherries and drinking water. Infectious hepatitis is an exhausting and very drawn-out sickness. Finally, Uncle Graef came and took me to his house. This was how the Lord provided me with a second mother and father. Gerti, their daughter, became my new "big sister." After work and on weekends Uncle Graef would sit by my bedside and read to me by the hour. He fed me with the patience of an angel until my appetite returned and my skin took on a normal color again. The Lord must have known that I needed a respite to generate new strength and courage.

"Praise the Lord for his wisdom and mercy, and all that is within me praise Thy Name!"

19: I must be in my Father's House

PSALM 122, 1: I am glad whenever they tell me, "We go to the eternal's house,"

I was declared healthy again and safe to return home. Reformation Day was approaching, falling on a week day. Any pupil who wished could get dispensation from school to attend church services. However, the pupil had to have a written note from his parent. My mother was not about to write one. I also had to bring one dollar to church for the collection. That meant either millions in old paper money or, since the currency just had been changed, one bill, or pennies, nickels or dimes. I approached my father with the latter subject first:

"Dad, I need one dollar for church." He took a new bill from his wallet and let it glide down to me. I would not have paper money, thinking that this was an old bill. I said, "I won't accept that, I want it in hard currency, pennies, nickels and dimes."

My father laughed. "Look at that sharp little woman ... she wants hard cash. Well, let me see what I can come up with!" He picked up the despised bill and put it where it had come from. Then he fished through all his pockets, letting me add up the coins to one dollar, filling both of my hands. I knew I was going to church. Now I told him that I needed a written statement for school. My father said: "Let your mother write the note."

"She will not do so."

"I don't make you go to church either."

"I know, but I am going to church, because that is where I must go!"

"Alright," he said, and set to write:

To the Elementary School,
to witness, My daughter Hildegard Lotz, has the urgent desire to attend church on Reformation Day, 1925, and is therefore not able to attend classes in the 3rd grade on the above day. Respectfully Yours,

Wilhelm Reinhard Lotz

On Reformation Day I delivered the note at school. Next

I owe my life to Jesus--You also?

I welcomed my friends on the way to church. I counted out my money to the penny ... none of the children had seen so much hard cash at any one time ... but I realized then that one bill would have done the trick. Christ must have smiled at all that seriousness about wanting to do my best. The Sunday School teacher was glad to get enough to provide a more prosperous Christmas for those children who truly had nothing.

Those were hard times. Only a third of my classmates owned shoes, and some of the girls did not own any underwear whatever. They were glad to have one dress and a coat, regardless of the fit. Wooden shoes, house slippers ... the majority wore rags on their feet.

This day the Lord had to comfort many, for the church was cold. "Lord, thank you for providing a warm school, where wet foot-rags can dry out on warm radiators." It was a prayer murmured by a boy my size in the seat behind me, and not meant for my ears. It hit me: was I not responsible for his being in church and not at school? I asked the teacher for permission to see the pastor. She shrugged her shoulders. I slipped out of the pew and went after the pastor. I caught him off guard: "Do you have a heated room empty in the parish house?"
"Yes? What about it?"
"Can you let our group meet in there for the rest of the day? You know, we are very cold!"
"I don't know whether you will fit into the room. Well, if you are very quiet and cooperative it may do. Promise?"
I led him to our group ... he counted 62 children and shuddered ... but he led us across the street. What joy and relief for many! In fact, no one thought of leaving at 1 o'clock. The teachers and the pastor took turns telling us stories and leading us in singing. Someone found hot milk and bread for those who had nothing for lunch.

Those were hard times. If Christ had lived then, he would have had to feed 5,000 every day.

20: You shall have a new body and eternal life

PSALM 88, 1-3:
> "O THOU ETERNAL,
> I cry for help in the day-time,
> and at night I moan before THEE...
> bend an ear to my cry.
> For trouble fills my body,
> my life is on the verge of death ...."

May 1926 brought on stomach cramps that would not leave me. My mother insisted I was fine, that I was just seeking her attention. Nothing was further from the truth ... I dragged myself around. Then the grapevine announced the coming of an unusually severe winter. It was the end of September when I supervised my gang in carrying leaves by the bushels for mulch to the top of my flower bed. It must have been covered by two feet of leaves everywhere. My mother was angry about it, but had no time to have them removed. Shortly thereafter I did not have the strength to go down the stairs.

I owe my life to Jesus--You also?

Dr. Stade was called. She listened to my mother and told her what she wished to hear: "Leave her in bed Friday and Saturday, get her dressed on Sunday, and Monday she can go back to school."

Sunday morning I was dressed. I went to the door; there I crumpled. Vaguely I heard my father ordering the maid to fetch the head surgeon. Dr. Spannhouse took one look at me and turned on his heels, saying, "I am getting the operation room ready, I am sending an ambulance. I give myself and the child two hours to save her life. Perhaps, with the Lord's help, we shall make it. I should have been called long ago."

It was November 12, at 11 A.M., when I arrived in the operating room and the struggle for life or death began. No crucifixion could have been worse. A ruptured appendix, gangreened in the last stages, peritonitis, part of a scissors lost inside, drainage tubes in all directions ... the devil had a field day for 30 days and nights. My body was raked with pain. I was on a constant, enforced fast, not even water ... my intestines had no place to send on the food. I was skin and bones; yet my stomach looked bloated like that of a woman in her ninth month.

My mother, writhe with remorse, sat at my bedside day and night. There was little anyone could do for me. No feeding, no moving, only reading ... "do you think she is sleeping?" They were counting the flies they had killed for having found their way into the putrid-smelling hospital room. The count stood at 106. The pastor came as always when he made the rounds. As he entered, my mother left. He always asked me for special wishes, and so he did today.
"Yes," I asked, "please read the Psalm with the shepherd ... I am going to meet him."
He nodded his head gravely. He pulled a chair, sat down and read: PSALM 23:
    "The LORD is my shepherd I SHALL NOT WANT ...

goodness and kindness wait on me, the eternal's guest within his household."

My spirit had left my body, thanks to His mercy. Once more I was free of all pains, feeling again strong on my feet. I left the dark behind me, and skipped toward the radiant light which shone before me. Then, out of the bright light came Jesus Christ walking toward me. At first He was gigantic in size, and as He came toward me He loomed in more human proportions. I hurried up toward him and He met me half way. The Lord took my hand in His. Jesus smiled, as if He wanted to say: "Now you are feeling well again, isn't it so!"

I smiled back: "Yes, thank you."

But then He turned my face away from the light and walked me leisurely back the way I had hurried up, and said:

"Your time has not yet come. I want you to accomplish many things yet. Now go back to your father. He is waiting for you."

I awakened and, to my utter surprise, my hands lay in my father's hands. I knew, things would be alright.

That moment my intestines had ruptured and all the pressure had stopped. I could breathe again, and eat once more.

Outside, winter had started in earnest. Temperatures kept plunging to an all-time low. At minus 31 Celsius it halted and would not budge. The school ran out of fuel and the radiators burst. It had to be closed for four weeks or longer. Water pipes burst even in the hospital. They had to chop the swans out of the pond to save their lives.

Five more major operations brought me through this terrible winter. In April, when the sun had ousted the winter and those birds who had survived thought of nesting, they put me into a carriage so I could have a look at the outside again.

All the gardens were ruined. Ancient chestnut trees,

hundreds of years old, had died; so had the apple trees and pear trees. Every shrub and flower in my mother's garden had been cut and burned.

I was anxious to know how my flower bed had fared. Absolutely beautiful! The chestnut leaves had proved a most complete shelter. The gardener was at work. He had carefully removed the leaves, and now he asked my permission to separate the clumps of bulbs, and divide root stock to replant my mother's garden.

That spring my dear grandmama became ill. I never was to see her again, but in our prayers we were very close. She prayed to the Lord: "Let the child live and take me home into your fold instead."

On May 28, 1927, I had my last operation ... no pains afterward. They brought the good news to Grandmama and she closed her eyes forever, happy to meet the Lord. Somehow, I knew the minute she was met by Jesus Christ, as He had met me, healed of all her pains and troubles. I knew she was alive.

In September I learned to walk again. It was a new beginning. I was no longer a child, though not yet an adult either. Would my mother change her attitude toward me? Would she accept me as an adult? Only time would tell. Meanwhile, I had my own bedroom, off limits to my brother. The year had made a difference, because my mother had sealed me off from all my friends. I shared none of their experiences, and they could not fathom mine. Church was not the same ... no one shared my experiences about Christ ... walking was still difficult, but ... no complaints. Then came the winter. Nonetheless:

> **"The Lord is my shepherd, I shall not want ... He leads me ... He revives life in me..."**

I could laugh again, for He had made me whole.

21: I know ... I get a home from God

2 CORINTHIANS 4, 7-9; 5, 1:

"But I possess this treasure in a frail vessel ... The transcending power belongs to GOD, not to myself; on every side I am harried but not hemmed in, perplexed but not despairing, persecuted but not abandoned, struck down but not destroyed ... I know that if this earthly tent of mine is taken down, I get a home from GOD, made by no human hands, eternal in the heavens."

A frail vessel I was. One would assume that one calamity was sufficent. Yet hardly two years later, on the first of Advent, I vomited blood and my urine ran red. It was one of those translucent sunny Sundays seldom seen. My father and I had planned a hike into God's world; he and I would be the only ones for breakfast. He was already seated when I entered ... my heart was racing. I took my seat and blanked out. When I came to, I lay on my bed, but every time I wanted to sit up my mind drifted away.

A physician was called ... a new man in town ... to a dying child. He dropped everything and hurried over ... up the fourteen steps and into my room at 10 A.M. on Sunday morning. This man had a receding forehead, the like of which I had not seen before, except, it was identical to the Greek statue of Amor at school that we used to decorate with disrespectful head gear. Here then, all of a sudden, Amor had sprung to life and was standing before me huffing and puffing. I had to laugh, and laughed so hard that it shook the bedstead, which used to be my father's. My father left my room in disgust. The doctor was peeved. He asked me with a stern voice:
"Have you vomited blood?" ... More laughter.
"Do you have pain?" ... "No." New laughter.
"Do you feel bad?" ... "No," laughter and hiccups.
Amor had done it to me. The doctor could not examine me; he could not take my pulse, because of the volcano that shook me. He took a specimen of urine, shook his

head, hardly looking at me, and promised my mother he would take the sample personally to the railroad station for the main laboratory. Meanwhile, he told my mother, "Let her have lots of eggs, in any form ... an egg-protein diet."

He left without a glance at me, but was cordial to my mother. My mother was truly furious. Then she came with eggs, eggnog, scrambled, cooked, fried, you name it, and I would not have any part of them. I had detested eggs ever since my bout with hepatitis. Besides, I was not hungry, and my father decided that fasting probably would be a lot better than overloading the stomach.

Dr. Eckhardt was a specialist in internal medicine and no fool. He neglected nothing. He had dispatched the specimen. He was briefed by telephone at 6:30 A.M. on Monday morning and asked casually: "Is the patient still alive? Kidney failure?"

Ten minutes later he rang our door bell till it stuck. The maid pushed the buzzer and left the door ajar. The doctor ran up the steps, brushed past the maid, nearly fell over the cleaning bucket, shouting: "I must see the child, I must see the child!"

My mother and father pulling on their housecoats rushed into my room after the doctor. He examined me, again demanding sharply: "Have you vomited blood?"

The Lord knew of it ... my mother, however, answered for me emphatically: "No, she has not vomited at all." Why should my mother not be right for once? My father looked at me quizzically ... then he asked the doctor:

"What if she had vomited blood?"

"We'd have to take her into the hospital and remove the disintegrating kidney."

"What chance do we have now, if she has not vomited blood?"

The doctor looked at him seriously and took his time. "She is in God's hands."

He studied the bucket of water at his feet. "The diet which I had given you yesterday, was completely wrong. They dictated to me a diet over the telephone ... no eggs or anything with albumin. Rice, vegetables, soup, no salt, and little sugar. She must have absolute rest. At best, it will take months. I shall see the child twice a week. A urine sample must be delivered regularly each day to the hospital. We'll keep you informed as to the changes."

He looked into my eyes again with his light. He shook his head, "such a report, and really no vomiting of blood?!" he muttered over me. "Well, we must take a chance and try it this way." Then he straightened out and added: "The decision should be out of my hands quite quickly. All depends on the tests. The second they show improvement she will have a chance. With God she'll make it."

He took along the morning specimen, convinced that his egg-diet was the worst ever he could have recommended.

There was improvement after the third day. I was not able to lift my head without fainting for fully three months. I lived the existence of a worm ... even Kafka could not have described it better. The diet was not at all undesirable: I saw my first oranges ... imported from Spain ... and tangerines from China. I had my first try at bananas. I had pigeon soup, and trout with lemon juice. My mother was an excellent cook!

The specimens steadily improved, and their number decreased. Even the doctor looked relaxed when he stopped in occasionally. I kept on growing like a weed. Finally I could hold up my head again, and the doctor declared the tests near normal. I learned to walk for the third time in my life.

With this new lease on life the hardest period ever was ushered in. It seems that the devil became concerned about the chance he could lose the bet made with the Lord before my birth.

22: You shall be blind for a time

PSALM 38, 18-22:
  **...For I confess my guilt, I sorrow for my sin. "Only,"
  I say, "let not my foes exult over me ... when I slip."
  For I am on the verge of collapse; my plight is ever
  present to my mind ... I intend to do good ... forsake
  me not, O THOU ETERNAL, be not far from me, O MY
  GOD; make haste to help me, to rescue me, O LORD!**

My body had been mended, and I could walk again. At
12 1/2 years of age I had reached my adult size. My mother
had been a good nurse, a calling that pleased her, despite
all adversities. But man cannot live by food alone. An avid
reader since I was six, I had read hundreds of books in my
solitude. I had been sealed off from the world and my peers
for nearly three years. I could hold a conversation with my
father and enjoy it. But what interested me was unknown to
my classmates, and therefore I was mocked and laughed at.
Women, those who had visited me when trying to comfort
me, those who had shared their problems with me so I
should not feel so singled out, knew me no longer. Now,
when I asked them how they were coming along, they could
not remember that they had anything happening to them
worthy of concern.

Christmas was no longer, but a commercial event; Easter
a good reason for a thorough house-cleaning. Christ was
nailed on the Cross ... Don't pride yourself with the
miserable good deeds you are able to do ... man is guilty
for having nailed him to the cross. You are man. You are
guilty just as every one else.

In truth, I fell without stumbling. I could walk again,
but one time in 400 steps my right leg just would not walk.
Without warning, regardless of whether I was on steps, in
class or in the middle of the street ... whenever the count
was up, I went down. I have never used more hose and
band aids during the rest of my life than I did in those
ensuing 2 1/2 years.

I was in trouble as it was. The school had regular
health inspection. The physical by a competent physician
was an annual event for everyone. I had missed it four
years in a row. Routine eye check: the doctor held my

right eye shut and asked me to read the letters on the chart.

"I see nothing."

"How many fingers?"

I guessed three. He opened the right eye, holding shut the left, and asked me to read the chart. I read even the finest print. I was blind in the left eye.

I was taken to the Eye-Clinic of the University of Jena, where a friend of my father, Professor Loehlein, was the leading specialist. It was established that I was blind, but not because something was wrong with the eye, but because the muscles were unused. Now the good eye had to be patched up, and, **ACTS 13, 11:**

"You shall be blind, unable for a time to see the sun." In a moment a dark mist fell upon me, and I groped about for some one to take me by the hands"

Teachers, adults, strangers, friends, everyone tried to educate me, and tell me what I must do to overcome my handicaps. I was not able to while away the time with reading. I compensated by studying science ... physics, chemistry, geography and astronomy, anything that could be memorized. Evolution took the place of "God created." I was taught etiquette ... that is, the forms, manners and ceremonies established by convention as acceptable and required in society. My mother insisted on this. Goodness and honesty was pressed into the mold to turn out an adult, convention could accept. Most teenagers accept it, because they are exposed to it long before, and gradually. I developed a fierce migrane headache.

ROMANS 2, 19-24:

"...If you are instructed by the law, persuaded that you are a guide to the blind, a light to darkened souls, a tutor for the foolish, a teacher of the simple, because in the law you have the embodiment of knowledge and truth -- Well then, do you ever teach yourself, you teacher of other people? You preach against stealing; do you steal? You forbid adultery; do you commit adultery? ... You pride yourself on the LAW; do you dishonor GOD by your breaches of the LAW?

Life, the life of an adult, was not worth living, my father did not care (or had nothing to say in the house), my body was garbage and all my mother's concentration and efforts were aimed at enhancing the outward appearance. God did not exist. How else could he tolerate such meaninglessness, suffering and insolence? Were his angels just an imagination of sick minds? One more temper tantrum and being told by my mother what I was thinking ... and I was standing on the window sill high above the iron picket fence ... to get it over with ... into the arms of Christ ... I did jump.

Verily, two angels of the Lord caught me and set me on the floor back inside in my room. I was dazed. There was a knocking. I felt lamed. The knock on my room door was repeated. Then my father's face peeked around the corner.

"Come, take off your patch, keep your glasses on, let's go for a walk, its such a nice day. Let's talk."

I took off the patch, put on the glasses and went.

"You see, God has created the world, and he has created everything which is in it. Evolution has its place. We were all born tiny and developed because of God's promise. We accumulate knowledge to prepare a better life for those who are to come after us. We are God's handymen and have to use the gifts he gave us in the cradle as best as we can. In studying chemistry, physics, and astronomy, new windows are opening for you to see how complex and vast God's creation is. This is giving the beholder more tools. Take astronomy. Undeniably, God has built into this universe a rhythm. It takes 24 hours, for instance, for the earth to turn about its own axis. He gave the sun and the moon and the stars their individual cycle. Certainly not without purpose. A lifetime is not sufficient to comprehend the greatness of God's creation, and there is no end to new discoveries. The Lord delights in us with every inquiry and with each new insight.

"There is a danger, however, that mediocre men freeze the meaning of the word, at whatever level of under- standing they have reached, and now wish to keep the world of God at their convenience, because they are lazy, vain and arrogant."

2 PETER 1, 9:

"Whereas he who has not these qualities by HIM is blind, shortsighted, oblivious . . ."

"I pity them, because they do not know what they are

missing. Man can be God's helper. Look for instance at this ant hill." We stopped in the middle of the high forest. "Here the forester has pegged a wire mesh over an ant nest to protect it from birds and adversaries, because he has observed that the trees within 50 yards of circumference from the ant hill will not be subject to diseases." The ant hill was almost shoulder high.

"This," my father continued, "is at the base of every profession. The doctor studies the body until he learns how God has constructed it most perfectly, and when something has gone wrong with it, he tries to be God's helper. It will not work without prayers. Neither will there be an end or a limit to the discoveries. Even I have hardly seen more than the beginnings. Unfortunately, all the wisdom you acquire cannot be passed on to the next generation. Our generation was blind and arrogant, which led to jealousy and war. **Guns and ammunition are the tools of Satan** and undoes what generations have achieved by following the Lord's commandments. God has placed a curse on weapons of any kind, for the wicked man fears those who are trying to do good."

1 JOHN 3, 1-2:

"You must not forget what a love the FATHER has for us, in letting us be called 'CHILDREN of GOD!' and such we are. The world does not recognize us? That is simply because it did not recognize HIM. We are children of GOD now ... what we will be? ... Like HIM -- at least then we will see HIM as HE is."

"By the way, I have talked with Loehlein," my father continued. "He is pleased with the progress your eye is making, he wants you in Jena for a battery of tests, and also will do everything to help you with the migrane headaches."

In one afternoon the Lord resolved all that which had piled up in my soul during the past four years. **He had not forsaken me,** He had sent his angels to rescue me, and ... He had sent my father to open up a new world, and show me a new way.

23: Oh heart, take courage!

2 THESSALONIANS 2, 2, 15-17:
"... I beg you not to let your minds get quickly
unsettled or excited ... stand firm and hold to the rules
... and may our LORD JESUS CHRIST himself and GOD
our FATHER, who has loved us and given us eternal
encouragement and good hope, graciously encourage your
heart and strengthen you for all good in deed and
word."

My blindness began to lift after the first four months;
then, from month to month, the thick lens grew thinner. It
was a slow process, with many trips to Jena. This time was
no exception: the moment the train was well out of sight of
the railroad station I was relieved of the migrane
headaches, and they would not return until the railroad
station came again into sight. I was resting between tests
at the eye clinic, when I realized this phenomenon. The
tests had never uncovered any abnormalities which could be
blamed. I was put through the Rorschach tests: when I
was supposed to see details, I saw the overall patterns,
and when I was to see overall patterns, I noted all the
details. They had fun working with me, and returned me
with a clean bill of health. I approached my hometown with
two pairs of new glasses, one for reading, and one for the
distance. When the train had passed a certain bend the
migrane headache began in all its severity. I talked aloud
in tongues, so that people thought I had popped.
"No, the devil, this has to stop immediately! Lord, what
is the matter with me!" I sat down and closed my eyes ...
"Fear to be a disgrace and a thorn in the eyes of your
mother ... Does it really matter what she thinks? ... Is it
not enough that I know you? ... what you are ... what
you will be? ... Don't I have faith in YOU?"

1 Corinthians 1, 27-28:

=50 =

I owe my life to Jesus--You also?

"GOD has chosen what is foolish in the world to shame the wise: GOD has chosen what is weak in the world to shame what is strong; GOD has chosen what is mean and despised in the world--things which are not, to put down things that are ... this is the GOD to whom you owe your being in CHRIST JESUS, whom GOD has made our 'WISDOM', that is our righteousness and consecration and redemption..."

I was rid of my migrane headache, which was never to return. I could face my mother; she was alright. She tried very hard to be master of everything herself. Whatever she was not able to handle, a goodly part of the chore, she tried to cover up.

Mother had a lovely mezzo-soprano voice. She had studied voice at the School of Music in Berlin, and was sought after for performances of church music, and a stand-in for operas and operettas. My father loved her dearly; he could sit at the piano for hours and accompany her. She was a very convincing actress, and it was a shame that she had to dramatize and act out all the hills and valleys which beset such a heterogeneous household ... at times frightening the wits out of its occupants, and then trailing off to the piano singing:

What refreshment for my senses, How envigorating for my heart, It runs through every vein, It quickens my very fiber, Wonderful refreshing feeling which fills me with new strength."

(Aria of Hanna from the Seasons by Haydn)

From now on, I could calm down the maids, not to take it so seriously, and tell my mother: "Let us take care of the problem! Go to the piano before you're hoarse." Somehow, that worked better for all concerned. A more preferable solution, however, was to be occupied outside the house.

24: Go feed my sheep!

CORINTHIANS 13, 11-12:
" ... When I was a child, I talked like a child, I
thought like a child, I argued like a child; now that I
am a man, I am done with childish ways. At present we
only see the baffling reflections in a mirror, but then it
will be face to face; at present I am learning bit by bit,
but then I shall understand as all along I have myself
been understood."

I wasn't a child any longer ... but somehow it is hard to
be done with childish ways. Perhaps it is I, who will never
be done with being a child ... for being a child means
growing and learning, preserving a willingness to do so.
That to me is the reason why God calls us "his children"
regardless of age. On the other hand, however, with all
the accumulated wisdom of sixty years, I continue to feel
inadequate to bear the burden of Christ's heir. At the time
I thought I was unique ... perhaps age-wise. Jesus Christ
remained the same.

In 1930 I signed up for the confirmation class with 85
other children. To our disappointment, the pastor was
nearer the nineties than the fifties. What mattered was not

the age, but that he did not know anything about the struggle of modern youth ... certainly not of this group before him, raised under so much deprivation and adversity, of this group of young people who had raised themselves with little adult supervision ... of these young people between 14 and 17 years of age, not compelled, but signed up on their own volition (with the exception of a small minority). This man had not ministered to a child for nearly two decades, since before the war. Now he could hardly justify his presence before 85 teenagers for three hours each week. He was used to talking with angels and archangels very sweet and saintly, of course in King James English. That was the language in which he addressed us, also.

On the way to the classes I was surrounded by a mob. Using my mother's techniques, I mimicked the dear old soul, matching his pathos, gestures, manner and word order in such a way that even the sparrows tumbled off the bushes for merriment.

Once started, there was no turning back. Inside, it turned into a heart-break. "Go feed my sheep!" We got petting only! Not nourishment ... what an opportunity lost! Cheap like "etiquette", something to satisfy the hypocrites, called "good citizens"; we were caught. In the end, the poor kept going, because it meant receiving their first adult suit or black dress, shoes, underwear and everything which went with it. To those who could not afford it, this was a donation from the congregation. The inflation was behind us, but such an outfit was out of the question for half of this class. The old pastor was petrified at the idea that some one could fail the public examination. Therefore, one whole season was occupied with the line-up, the word order, and the actual questions. Everything was staged a hundred times, and rehearsed, word for word.

Confirmation classes were projected over two years. At the end stood the feared public examination on one Sunday,

I owe my life to Jesus--You also?

confirmation on Palm Sunday, and the Lord's Supper on Thursday before Easter. If you will imagine a drill master approaching you in Shakespearian English, or this group of 85 ... well, it is useless. At last, each one of us received a piece of paper with the long practiced personal instructions (lest we should forget!) with the three questions we would be asked, by whom, and the correct answers. We were told to bring the paper along, just in case we had forgotten the answers. The line-up was alphabetical, and, though the youngest, my place was in the middle because of L. Three of us were called together before the council in front of the congregation, and no one had a mishap, or failed, I assure you! We were dressed in our finery, and did not recognize each other. Clothes made a difference!

I was wretched. Because this was my confirmation, imagine, 450 gifts had streamed into our house, some forty azaleas plus other Easter arrangements.

On Palm Sunday our church was filled to its rafters. My father and brother, however, were absent. Both shared a room in the hospital, they both suffered from kidney stones and both were in severe pain.

By now I was truly fed up with this farce called confirmation; my conscience was rankled because now, after the ceremonies had already begun, we were suddenly asked to give testimony of our faith, confirming, agreeing, and dedicating.

This was commercialism, a meaningless performance to please the public. It was rigged to cover up the justified fear and suspicion that they had failed to get the basics across. I was revolting against the superficiality of these rites.

At that point, the pastor intoned the question: "Any one, who has reservations and doubts, and feels he or she cannot agree with the teaching of the church, or feels the

afraid rather than reassured.

Before, my hands were made for rough tough work; now they had finger tips to feel with, for guidance and seeing. I taught knitting and crocheting better than those who could see. I could do bead work, as long as some one told me which box held what color. Of course, my school work suffered some more, but my mind was sharpened to remember the sequences in mathematics, and I could add in my mind quite correctly the first time over. Where once I was at the bottom of a class of 35, I soon headed the class as the third or fourth. And ever after, I could tell what was going on without turning to look.

When I could see again plainly, everything looked so much more colorful, and today I still have my joy in combining touch, hearing and seeing with an awareness of Christ's never ending mercy in turning calamity into an asset, even a treasure. I learned a great deal during those years about music, appreciating beautiful instruments and voices. Of course, it also left me over-sensitive when submitted to poor quality instruments, but one can avoid such exposure without getting upset. Noise in all walks of life is part of finding one's way around; in time, occupation, of location, but it is not music. Music has a transcendental quality expressing mood and feeling, it reveals the inner drive about what one strives to attain. Music is like speaking in tongues, when you don't know exactly what it is that you want, or what is good for you, but it is in the end resolved in Jesus Christ. This is the way He is feeding us.

Each day to me is a new lease on life, with new impressions and new surprises, new revelations and new challenges. Very little has changed ... Christ is still the same.

26: I am with you in the Spirit

EPHESIANS 4, 4-6:
 "For there is one body and one spirit ... one LORD, one
faith ... one GOD and father of all, who is over us all,
who pervades us all, who is within us all."
COLLOSSIANS 2,5: "...For although I am absent in body
I am with you in SPIRIT."

Bonn was a sleepy university town ... the town where
my mother had grown up ... I was visiting my grandmother. I should have relied on no one but Jesus Christ
... probably we were much alike, but we should never have
the chance to discover each other ... my mother's opinion
stood between us. (Parents, bias is learned in the cradle,
right or wrong, it inhibits the thinking of your children.
My mother was good to her mother, but there was a
generation gap, passed on to us.)

However, my grandmother had a lovely friend, Aunt
Johanna Henry. Her soul was as pure and spotless as the
spirit of Jesus Christ. She was a devout Catholic, while our
branch of the family was Protestant. They were friends
since marriage, hardly out of their teens; they loved and
treasured each other dearly. Aunt Johanna and I loved each
other at first sight. Despite almost total blindness she
taught English, French, and Mathematics, preparing
students for board examinations. She was always cheerful
despite mountains of adversities. I adopted her as my
mother and she accepted me as her child. Her bed was the
only one I ever shared, and we could talk all night about
our experiences, about Christ Jesus, belief, and faith.

It truly did not matter that we seldom had the
opportunity to see each other ... we could communicate,
nevertheless. This was augmented, or confirmed by an
occasional note ... there was no generation gap between us
despite thirty some years.

This was confirmed at various occasions. When I obtained
a scholarship to study in England, the permit to leave the
country came suddenly. Neither of us had a telephone. I
arrived very late that night. My heart skipped a beat ...
her house door was unlocked. I opened it noiselessly, but

let the door snap shut into the lock. Her voice chirped from above: "Is it you, Hildelein, I left the door open for you ... make sure it is locked."

"Yes, beloved, it is I, it's locked now. How did you know I was coming?"

She laughed: "How did you know the door was open? I knew you were on the way since noon."

In the Lord, anything is possible. Mother and daughter, we had only one night to pour out our love and share and sustain each other. At eight in the morning I was back at the railroad station.

I was in England ... I had a very busy schedule ... for the first time as a member of an older teen-age crowd! It was August 10, when I dreamed I was back with grandfather. I sat on his bed with him, he was in trouble. All that day I wept at the slightest provocation. In spirit, I recited to him all the good times we had had, bowling together with his friends, the feeding of the bees, watching the swallows, and helping the pigeons. Then, around five o'clock in the afternoon, I turned very quiet. A sigh welled up in me, and a sob. "Thank you, dear Lord, for loving him."

Seconds later, I snapped out of it completely, and I participated happily in everything as usual. In the morning I received a telegram.

"Wednesday, August 10, at 5 P.M. your grandfather went home to the Lord, Your grieving Father."

Maude Brown took me into her arms. "That must make you feel very sad."

I shook my head: "No, he is relieved of all his troubles today ... yesterday was a rough day for him..."

She let go of me, "you are a strange child." She draped my coat and jacket sleeves with a black band, to let every one know that I had lost a loved one.

Revelation 22, 5: Night there shall be none;
they need no lamp or sun to shine upon them,
for the Lord God will illumine them;
and they shall reign for ever and ever.

=59 =

27: The covenant

EZEKIEL 22, 3-7:
>"So I leave you to the scorn of the nation ... you
>infamous nation, seething with disorder ... the
>leaders of Germany ... have been overbearing, bent
>on bloodshed ..."

I loved my hometown and all the familiar soil at the foot
of the Harz Mountains, and all the people I knew within the
whole region. From the Mountain Of Our Lady all the land
stretched before my feet. Everything basked in the sunshine. Three baby deer played not far away, their parents
munching the juicy grass, their ears tuned to the bluejay
and the cuckoo for warning signals. The grasses were
blooming, their heads nodding in the light breeze. The
sounds of bells drifted in the wind and mingled with others
to announce the second hour in the afternoon.

I drifted off and had a vision: "I saw soldiers on skir-
mishes with helmets and guns in their hands, bombs falling

over the hometown, destroying, killing, maiming, wiping out the theater, schools ... it was burning downtown. When the dust settled everything began to decay, our house was still standing, but the eaves of the roof had been perforated enough to count the stars through them. The people were neglected, the forgotten ones of the war."

"Lord," I cried, "don't show me anymore ... what will become of my father, my mother, my brother?"

Again I saw bombs falling, I was choking in the dust. I was completely enshrouded in smoke, or fog. I screamed: "Don't destroy them, don't destroy every one I love!" Then I saw the sun break forth, and tall lilies. I saw my father, mother and brother safe and sound in surroundings I knew nothing of.

And the Lord said: "I will take you out of this country when the time is ripe," and with that I woke up. I had disturbed the deer; they were prancing away from me.

What rubbish! How could my mind be filled with such thoughts? I tried to shake it ... I looked about me, the sun was warm, the bees hummed, the deer browsed again, a colibri sipped on nectar.

"Lord, why would you want to destroy this earth?"

"Why did men wish to crucify me? Why does a mother not trust her daughter?"

"Lord, you have the power to change man's mind, if you so desire!"

"I have only power over those who do believe in me, I will be with you to the end of your days, and then you will be with me forever!"

I folded my hands in my lap and pondered His words. This was May 1934.

28: Christ sustains those who obey Him

DEUTERONOMY 29, 27-28; & 29, 20-21:
"...That was why the ETERNAL'S anger blazed against
this country, bringing on it every curse in this book;
... in anger, in fury, in heavy wrath, the ETERNAL
will blot out his name ... and single him out ... for
doom..."

Gerhart Penzler was my neighbor; orphaned during the
First World War, he was raised across the street by his
grandparents. I don't think he ever knew his grandmother
well. She had passed away, and Lotte, his mentally
retarded aunt, cared for the household in her way. He was
older than I and had graduated from high school. He then
had been drafted into the work corps, a requirement for
entrance into the university. He was on furlough, stationed
somewhere in the North.

As old neighbors, we had shared much, before. Now he
appeared in my hiding place ... his heart was troubled,
and lonely as I; his grandfather was too old to know what
was going on outside the house. We sat in the grass
together like sister and brother ... if he had other
motives, it surely was not revealed to me. He took my
hand: "Hildegard, there are things going on here inside
this beautiful country which are pure hell on earth. Think
of it, I am so sick of the things I had to witness. Believe
me, most of the fellows in my outfit feel that way. Imagine,

we are detailed to dig graves, and to guard a barbed wire
compound, far away from any town. Inside human beings
like you and I, are herded. Every day they bring more of
them by the truck loads ... No one feeds them, men,
women, children, all ages. They stick their bony arms
through the fence, at best whimper, look at us with huge,
hollow eyes. We slip them our sandwiches ... but what does
one mean for so many? If any one catches us, we are shot
on the spot. They caught two just the other day. I tell
you, it haunts me in my sleep."

He meant to say much, much more. He was informed of
what was going on here at home, also. My father, as so
many, was hunted down because he loathed the government.
Would they succeed and take him to the same place?

One of my mother's brothers had fled to Switzerland ...
not that my family had Jewish blood in its veins; being
against the regime was sufficient. True, they had more
than one reason to hate my father. He had a childhood
friend, Ernest Langenbach, who was as dear to his heart as
his own brother. But that was not the issue. My father
despised the government for twisting the law to their
advantage ... the "Water Gate Gang" had found favor in
the eyes of the police and the labor unions. The mayor of
our town had been an embezzler and arsonist, sprung out
of jail. My father was to them John the Baptist alive:

MATTHEW 3, 7-9:
"You brood of vipers, who told you to flee from the
coming wrath? Now, produce fruit that answers to your
repentance, instead of presuming to say to yourselves:
'We are of German blood' ... I tell you: ... the axe is
already at the root of the trees; any tree that is not
producing good fruit will be cut down and thrown into
the fire."

They looked at my father in the same way as they did
John the Baptist. His friends came from all over the

country to hear my father's opinion. They heard him talk not only in the woods and in the fields, but also at school and in the market square. He condemned them in Greek, Latin and French. He was not even diplomatic about it. They stalked after him with a passion.

One day I came home from school and found two Nazis planted in the foyer. My mother stood near the kitchen door weeping, the maid scared to death on the far side. I asked: "What brought you here?"

"We are to pick up Dr. Wilhelm Lotz for interrogation!" Heels cracked as they stood at attention. That, then, was the reason for the limousine at the door ... hmm, that was not reason enough for my mother to weep. I looked at her sharply asking softly: "Is Dad in the house?"

She wept all the more and shook her head.

"Alright, gentleman, why not search the house."

I have seldom seen cats pounce with more alacrity upon certain prey, than those two henchmen searching for my father. They climbed into the wardrobe, they virtually crawled underneath the king-sized beds, and felt in all the cabinets. I led them into the attic and finally into the coal cellar, where they actually started shoveling into the pile of coal. I stopped them.

Meanwhile I had also found out why my mother was weeping. My father had come home from teaching because he had been struck by terrible pain in his war-injured hip. She had sent for an ambulance, and now he was in the operating room in the hospital ... the safest place to be under the circumstances. I had egged on those two henchmen, playing for time. They looked dirty and disheveled, and not at all in keeping with the limousine outside. I told them: "Believe me, my father has never been known to hide himself from any one, he is much too honorable. He is not here, he was picked up by an ambulance about twenty minutes before you drove up. He is now in the operating room for an emergency operation ... why not clean yourselves, drive to the hospital and verify my claim. But please come back here and let us know."

They did drive to the hospital and, of course were told that visitors were not permitted. They returned to the house a couple of hours later:
"Sorry for the commotion, we verified your claim. He is in the hospital. We reported it to headquarters, and effected a dropping of the charges. Heil H.___!" Heels clicked, they turned and marched down the stairs in parade step. The eager beavers had dealt with the case efficiently. That was the first of five incidents, wherein Christ averted misery, for I loved my father.

Unless personally involved, one did not know about the conflict and the power struggle. If you wished to eat, live, and go to the university, you had to keep quiet. Gerhart Penzler knew that he risked his life and the lives of those he confided in, should his story become known. By isolating the individual and insisting that each person minds his own affairs, the Nazis could rule the country, and get away with murder. Being well informed when the presses are biased and censored (or preoccupied with trivia) is difficult. People must try to assert their freedom by caring for their fellow men, feeling responsible for their youth, in particular.

The economic conditions all around us improved. The farmers again made a living. The vagrants who had lined the streets and used to assemble at the corners had disappeared. The aged received sufficient pensions, even enough to enjoy a few of the amenities. People found work for decent wages. For once in my life-time children had enough to eat ... and sported sturdy shoes. Even the milk program at school folded. The shelves at the grocers were fully stacked at reasonable prices. Five bills were substituted by a shiny piece of silver. For once there was enough currency in circulation for every one.

29: For the Lord none are dispensable

1 PETER 5, 8-9:
"Keep cool, keep awake. Your enemy the DEVIL prowls like a roaring lion, looking out for someone to devour. Resist him; keep your foothold in the faith, and learn to pay the same tax on suffering as the rest of your brotherhood throughout the world."

My dream was to become a doctor, and in due time I left home for the children's clinic on the Harz Mountain. I was still under 18. The hospital had an acute shortage of every type of staff, and every spare moment was occupied in one capacity or other. Deaconesses ran the institution like clockwork, with every minute accounted for: work, meals, prayers, class work, study period, you name it. There was no room for emergencies.

I was assigned to the children's ward, where there was a little boy, named Heini. Heini was to stay in bed, but Heini was everywhere except where he should have been; he was into everything.

The painter had just finished painting the porch sky blue. He had closed the door to the children's ward, and asked for them to stay out until it was dry. But Heini went onto the porch and stuck his fingers into the wet paint, drawing all over the wall. I discovered him, and took him to the bathroom, cleaned his hands with turpentine, and told him: "If you do that again the devil will catch you and punish you."

It had been a sweltering hot day in August. Suddenly clouds darkened the sky, and a brilliant flash of lightning with a deafening clap of thunder shook the earth. For a fraction of a minute everything was quiet ... then, a piercing scream from the porch ... I ran ... crumpled at the strike ... it was Heini. One light spot, one blue finger!

"I won't do it again, I won't do it again, I promise, I promise!" I knew he would keep his promise this time ...

Tragedy struck the hospital. A little boy was admitted with a fever and a cold. I helped the student nurses with the extra load, I fed him and bedded him at various times during the following days. One by one, all the nurses who cared for him turned sick with a cold. The others divided the load and I too worked overtime. My room mate took sick, and was fed aspirin, but otherwise she was neglected. On the second day her throat was visibly swollen; on the third day I could not contain myself any longer, I played doctor, commanded her to open her mouth and pressing the tongue down with a spoon, I saw that it was white. I washed my hands, turned on my heels, ran out of the hospital, and hailed a taxi.

My mother and I had a private physician in town, I persuaded the man to drop everything, paid him for the house call in advance. He did follow me into the taxi, and to the bedside of my room mate.

The man lost no time. Within the hour, my room mate, three other student nurses, the little boy, all were removed by ambulance to another hospital with an isolation ward. Diphtheria was on the rampage ... even I proved to be too late to save any of those five.

Those who were left had to double and triple their workload. I missed meal time a couple of times, and was sent to Sister Maria Magdalena in the kitchen. She belonged to the hierarchy of the hospital. She tried to start a conversation: "Don't imagine you could save the hospital by working a 14 hour day. If they die? ... all men are dispensable ... when one drops out, the Lord will send another one."

I owe my life to Jesus--You also?

Such callousness from a woman of the cloth! That stung ... I stayed in touch with the doctor. He held no hope. That week four student nurses between nineteen and twenty-five were buried. We were not told, ever. Outside of myself no one knew; none of the others asked.

When their relatives came gathering up their belongings they found out the truth.

In my weariness, I asked the Lord: "Why have You left me to carry on. Truly, why have I been spared the disease?"

And He spoke to me: **"You are immune to diphtheria, because your mother had diphtheria before you were conceived."**

All occupants in the hospital were vaccinated, including all the patients. But by that time I was already dismissed from the hospital because of insubordination, that is, summoning an outside physician without permission.

At home I asked my mother about diphtheria. "Oh yes, while your father was in the war I worked in the field hospital and contracted diphtheria of the womb, losing my first baby. A half a year later you were underway."

No one is dispensable in the eyes of the Lord. No one has the licence to neglect and tempt Him recklessly. However, the Lord's ways are not the ways of the world, and my removal from the hospital was one way to let me know that He had other things in mind for me. Sister Maria Magdalena was right in her way. The hospital filled a need, it did not collapse; but the Sisters were ousted and the Brown Shirts took over.

My action saved many others, just then exposed.

30: Crippling is not necessary

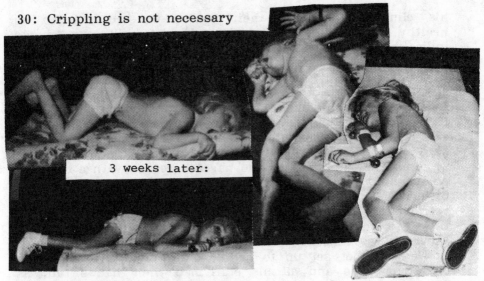

3 weeks later:

2 CORINTHIANS 7, 3-4, and 6:

"I am not saying this to condemn you. Condemn you? Why, I repeat, you are in my very heart, and you will be there in death and life alike. I have absolute confidence in you, I am indeed proud of you, you are a perfect comfort to me, I am overflowing with delight, for all the trouble I have had to bear ... But the GOD who comforts the rejected comforted me by the arrival of ..."

I was accepted at the University of Berlin. I signed up to absolve the internship along with the class work. After two weeks of terrifying experiences, I was assigned to an elderly obstetrician needing additional help for his outpatient clinic, which had started out as a hobby. Here I was to **teach parents with movement-handicapped babies how to get them started in life, to grow up normal, and preventing them from becoming crippled. The word cerebral palsy was never used.** This was a fun job, though time-consuming. The old doctor had quite a clientele. Other obstetricians and former students referred those parents to his clinic as soon as their babies were discharged as healthy from the hospital. We had to fill our charts indicating the degree of movement-handicap, which he checked, and then teach the parents what to do at home. In general we saw only the mothers with their babies, sometimes grandmothers. During the period of a year we must have taught over 125 parents most successfully. His files covered over 20 years. Only a few victims managed to slip through. Perhaps the parents were convinced that their baby was alright, or that their doctor thought it was unnecessary. I saw only two parents return with a cerebral palsy child of two and three years of age, complaining bitterly that nothing had been done. Then he would retrieve the record from his file and show them the paper they had signed despite his insistence that their child was "severely movement-handicapped."

We were not set up to handle older children; and as an obstetrician he and all his staff had their hands full. At any rate, my days were filled to the brim. For unknown reasons, holidays were a special cause for doubtful delight. It mattered little which holiday. As soon as one third of the staff was on vacation babies decided to arrive. The delivery rooms were overcrowded. As you may have guessed, babies defy scheduling for birth. All hands were tied up in the delivery room. Normally we delivered 9 babies per day, but on holidays we would have to deliver 18 babies. Who'd want to turn them back? Each one of us stuck it out until relief returned from vacation ... 32 hours on our feet. **NO ONE WAS DISPENSABLE!** We were a close knit team, doctors, laboratory staff, nurses and clean-up personnel. We were there to make the mothers happy in their hour of need. So many gifts poured in that we decorated the whole station to look like a flower shop, lasting for several weeks ... and all the glowing faces! That paid for all the effort.

Exams were scheduled for the week before Christmas. With seven days to spare, I had a dream at night: "My father was in bed immobile. My mother was weeping; his food untouched. And this is what the Lord said: "Go home to your father, you are the only one who can give him courage to carry on!"

I checked the morning mail. A letter from my mother ... everything was in order, nothing unusual! I ignored the dream. The following night I dreamed the identical dream. That was upsetting. But I had no leisure time to let it carry me away. No letter from home, but then, I could not expect two letters in a row. The third night again I had the same dream. That demanded heeding. As soon as morning had come, I made the rounds to every member of the examination committee: "Yes, under the circumstances you can take your exams beginning tomorrow." Said and done ... as soon as I had finished I took the night train arriving at home at seven o'clock in the morning.

When I entered my parents' bedroom, the scene was identical to the one in the dream: My mother was sitting on his bed weeping, his food untouched, my father lying immobile. He had learned that he had inoperable cancer near the hip and the spine, on the place he had been injured in the war. He was in pain, and did not want to live.

Mercy killing ... well, he asked for the impossible ... I was alive, why would the Lord want to let him die? I had hardly shed hat and coat, when the others left us alone. My presence had aroused his curiosity. "How did you find out? I wanted it to be finished by the time you came home. Has mother notified you?"

"No, there was no way she could have done so!" When I had told him, he looked at me in utter disbelief. I called for soup, and he sat up, a little weak and shaky after the five day fast. He ate with a healthy appetite whatever I offered him.

1 Corinthians 16, 14:
Let all you do be done in love.

31: HE protects and preserves your life

PSALM 12, 1 & 7-8:
> **"The eternal will guard you from all harm HE will preserve your life; HE will protect you as you come and go, now and for evermore."**

Father left right after Christmas for the clinic in Frankfurt a/Main. That was January 1937. The train had hardly pulled out of the station, when the Nazi van drove up to our house to pick him up for interrogation. That looked like a one way trip. Christ had spared him that. I left for Berlin.

Shortly before Easter recess I received a letter from my father, that he was able to leave the clinic for home. He sent me the instructions: "Let us meet in Erfurt and ride the shuttle together. This is only possible if you board the first section of the express from Berlin, I include the schedule. Note, the second section will be 15 minutes too late, and would mean two hours and a half of waiting till the next one."

Of course! I carried his letter with the instructions in my coat pocket. Dressed in latest fashion, I had arrived on the platform in plenty of time. The first section was already waiting with the engines primed. I went up and down the first section, and could not be persuaded to board it.
Finally the whistle blew, the doors were closed and the train moved slowly out of the station. I shook my head: what foolishness. The second section moved up to take its

place ... I climbed into a middle section and claimed a place at the window. It was crazy. I knew the instructions, and yet, I had done exactly the opposite. No chance of making connection! That would be hard on father ... ridiculous.

Nevertheless, I felt aglow all over. The ride was uneventful. The train, as always, made good time. By 1 P.M. we passed the Leuna plant before Halle when the train began to slow to walking speed. It stopped. It moved half-heartedly. The conductors let down the steps and hung out to get a glimpse of the obstruction. We could have milked the cows in the meadow. The train walked a mile or so, and stopped, then a second one ... we had just about reached the huge bend. Finally we got a view of the disaster. The train began tacking across a dozen switches reserved for freight trains. We had to circumnavigate the wreckage of the first section strewn all over the inside of the bend. We threaded our way out safely.

Meanwhile, true to his instructions, my father waited for the **first** section. Of course, he was upset, sitting for him was difficult, and walking was painful. The shuttle was missed. Stretching out was another three hours away. He consulted the bulletin board:

"Express from Berlin delayed: 10 Minutes."
He went back into the waiting room. Then the loud-speaker announced: "20 minutes delay". The half hour had ticked off. Still no train. Then, ten minutes later, my train pulled to a halt. The numbers of the train did not match those on the schedule. Nevertheless, as promised, he was waiting at the right place for the middle section. When the door opened I stepped right into his arms.

Father took me into the dining room for a lovely supper. We had so much to share, I thought nothing about it until he opened the paper at breakfast, showing the accident and explicitly stating that it was **the first section** of the Express from Berlin.

with Christ, anything is possible!

32: I am the way

JOHN 21, 15-16:
"... Do you love me?"
--"Why, LORD, you know I love you..."
--"Then be a shepherd to my sheep..."

Had I not known Christ until teen age, I would not have had a reason to seek the church. Considering my confirmation instructions, my experiences as an adult in the congregation would not have been incentive enough, and probably would have precluded any active interest. According to my mother, the clergy ranked with the saints; in my father's opinion, spineless; and as to my experience? Well, I pitied them: may the Lord give them wisdom!

When I was fifteen I had joined the Luther Academy as a regular member; I avoided stating my age. Theologians gathered from all over the world, from Poland, Finland, Sweden, Australia, from England and the U.S.A. Because of my knowledge of English, I was accepted as a hostess for foreign students. I gladly participated in all the lectures and read the required books and material. I sat in on private discussion groups held by famous leaders of the church such as Bishop Maharends, Professor Bultmann, Bishop Lilie, and Dr. Martin Niemoeller, in which each propounded his theories on the Bible and the on-going problems of the church. It was my duty to take notes wherever I went, to be able in turn to explain to the foreign participants what was under discussion. From hand to the mouth, I passed on what I had just learned myself. I, who never had owned my own Bible, marvelled most about the great wisdom and understanding pertaining to Christ's kingdom.

When first I went to Berlin, I made a great detour to Bonn to see Aunt Johanna, then I stopped in Eberfeld /Barmen to see Pastor Niemoeller at his home. He had just served his first stretch in prison, and the government was waiting for his next move before locking him up again. No one hindered me; dressed elegantly, I walked past men standing in front of the house ... I rang the bell. The buzzer opened the door and I walked up to his flat, five flights above the street. Again I rang the bell and asked to see "the famous man of God."

It was his wife ... she mumbled an excuse and said: "He is not at home," and shut the door.

I rang again. This time he, himself, opened the door, dressed in a house coat, but let me only into the vestibule from where one could see the street below.

"Child, what do you want from me?"

I did not know what I wanted from him, as truly as I was standing before him, believe me, nothing worthwhile came out of my mouth.

He led me to the window and pointed out those men I had passed. "They are there to spy on me. Any one I receive is suspect. You, too, will become suspect as my agent, or as an agent of Christ, whom they fear. Your presence here just creates more difficulties all around."

By this time, Christ had put words into my mouth: "What body of Christ then can I join to learn more about HIM and about the living church"

"Here in Germany there is no safe place ... all his workers are suspect. The only place which is still able to function is the Burckhardt-House in Berlin/Dahlem." He gave me an address and literature, but made me hide it. He opened the door. I closed it again. I had come for sustenance: "Let's say a prayer."

He hesitated...? Then he closed his eyes, he recommended this young thing before him into the hands of the Almighty. Then he heaved a sigh of relief, opened the door and let me out. He stood at the head of the stairwell and watched me wind my way down the stairs shaking his head, and wiping his forehead.

"That was a strange detour, Lord! Let's see what the Burckhardt-House is like." With that I embarked for Berlin.

33: Fear not, Jesus fight our battles

2 CHRONICLES 32, 7-8:

>"Be firm," he said, "be brave, be not daunted nor dismayed for Adolf Hitler or for all his host: we have with us <u>ONE</u> greater than all he has; he has a mortal force, but we have with us the ETERNAL OUR GOD to help us and to fight our battles."

The Burckhardt-House was run by women theologians for women who wished to train for the Lord's work. They had come from everywhere, willing to be commissioned to anywhere to fill a need. If at a church, for instance, a pastor was stopped in the middle of his sermon and dragged to prison, a woman was ready to walk right into his pulpit and pick up where he had left off.

Women carried on. Churches built for 200 people were filled with an overflow of another 800. Loud-speakers were set up outside in the snow.

Pastor Niemoeller came to preach a stint in a church in Dahlem, a Wednesday evening series, until it was forbidden to hold church on Wednesdays. Thursdays were not mentioned in the order ... so be it Thursday evenings. Then all evenings were on the blacklist and we'd meet at 6 A.M. A number of times they had a warrant for the pastor's arrest, but the crowd was so dense that they could not reach him during the services. Of course, after the services no one could tell where he was to be found. That was the naked truth, he was lost in the crowd. The grapevine was much faster than posters, or radio broadcasts, we had just to state time and place and the crowd was there, often at less than 4 hours notice.

I was detailed to help in a youth group for Bible studies, nothing else was permitted. A detachment of 35 Nazis were dispatched to monitor that. We welcomed them like every one who came. 45 round tables were set up in a large hall. Each table held twelve people. Bibles were laid out. We distributed the monitors, one to each table; each table had at least one trained teacher and ten students. Monitors and pupils were treated completely equal. He received a Bible like every one else. How could he judge what we were using if he could not, or would not open it? This was first hand information from the best source! Once read for himself, he could judge whether or not the discussion centered about the Bible only! Was that not the purpose of his being here? Every one wore name tags, however, the first name only, and the monitor was one of the group. There were tags of various colors. Yellow stood for those children with special needs. Red was chosen by those who wished to be baptised, and green for those to be confirmed. Nobody of course, paid any attention to the colors the monitors had chosen, because they did not receive the written instructions given to the others. It took but minutes and each table felt like one big family. Every one participated, asking questions and contributing. Meager refreshments made the rounds.

Unknown to the monitors, a large number of youngsters had come on regular basis against the express will of their parents. A goodly dozen had no place to go, denounced and disinherited by their families, because of their belief in Christ; their parents were of Jewish faith. There were no other motives: for the State it was "blood" not "faith" which counted. These children had selected their own Christian name. Each table had one or two of them, indistinguishable from the others. All were regulars.

Most of the assembly at my table had attended every meeting and had come for baptism, right in front of the monitor. Some had memorized the New Testament by heart, chapter by chapter, so that no one could take away the WORD from them. The ordained women took over those tables ... it looked like play-acting ... the candidate knelt and repeated by heart as instructed. Certificates were handed out. Not that I remember a disturbance during the meeting itself.

During my two years in Berlin this group sent no less than 200 Christians like that from age eight to seventeen to sister congregations in France and England. Mostly converts, or suddenly without a family.

The joy and pride among the attendants were our monitors. As long as it was possible, they turned up regularly. Of course, we never wrote them out a certificate, but we knew Christ took care of them. To insure their return, they had to do something drastic to uphold the party-line. They were comical, because at the end of each evening, they would jump up for a blistering rap session. They censored us for using whatever the name for the session. They forbade us to use the same passages for the next meeting. They ranted at the Church ... they trumpeted the names of those Christians newly imprisoned, as reliable as a new press release, written hot from the wire. They "warned" us against fraternizing with the newly released prisoners, telling us often where and when (which enabled us to grab a taxi and rush to pick them up). They put on a frightful show sounding so downright horrible that some of the children put their fingers into their ears to shut

=78 =

them out. When that was done each monitor would give his teacher a handshake, jump into formation yelling: "Heil Hitler", and then made us clear the hall in a jiffy, waiting at the door till the last one had left and the lights were switched off.

There was no loitering. The children ran and dispersed. We knew the Nazis had no choice ... and the worse they carried on, the more likely they had a chance to attend the next meeting. Each child knew the risks in coming and going, just in being labeled a Christian. What they had memorized could never be confiscated. I have not met an **individual** Nazi. A lone man never will rise against a Christian, much less against the Lord. Like any mob they dare to proceed boldly. They wiped out denominationalism: Lutheran, Reformed, Anglican, Greek Orthodox, Baptist, Catholic. With one stroke it mattered only that we were children of Jesus Christ, our Lord. We were proud to wear a fish, or any other symbol which identified us, and let each other know whom we could trust. It was the admission of faith that we belonged to the militant church.

Each and every meeting was used by members and, also, by the adversaries to spread the news about the well-being of individual members. Dispatchers informed the grapevine, and before work the crowd waited at bus stations, and subway entrances for the latest information. They came quietly and they went quietly. They trusted each other: Revelations 4,1:
"We knew only those who were hot or cold (who would take a stand for, or against CHRIST). Those who were luke warm stayed at home, there was not merit for them to risk their hide.

34: But they who trust in Me shall live

ISAIAH 57, 1, 3, 12-13:

"Meanwhile the good man dies, and no one heeds it; pious men are perishing, and no one cares. The Evil of the day kills off good men; they enter peace ... step forward, you, you sons of sorcery, brood born of harlots and adulterers: at whom are you jeering, at whom are you sneering, putting your tongues out? ... But I will expose your doings ... your loathsome idols, when you cry, will bring you neither help nor gain ... But they who trust in ME shall hold the land and own my sacred hills."

I was busy with classes to attend, the laboratory, teaching parents to overcome the handicap of their children, and doing duty in the maternity wing. Flowers, gifts of all kinds and for all occasions streamed our way. We supplied the shut-ins, the poor, and the lonely, with little delights. That which had no takers I took to the little waifs stranded with no place to go, hidden in the attic or cellar of the Burckhardt-House.

That I was left unmolested for nearly two years was a miracle in itself. I lived in a student home, my pals a

tightly knit group of nine students, who were hard at work
likewise. Indoctrination meetings were mandatory. We had
assigned seats. I made a good move by volunteering for
press photographer, since I owned the equipment. They
were delighted. Friends of mine loved to use the equipment.
That was an ideal set-up! My equipment went listening to
the endless speeches, and rallies, while I went about my
business. Each night at curfew time my equipment and I
met within the four walls of my room. Sometimes it was
waiting for me with exposed films sitting next to the door,
inside, or, at other times was set inside after I had turned
in already.

Eventually, however, they must have missed me at the
meetings. They started to interrogate us periodically. That
was very treacherous: Unknown to each other we were
privately "interviewed". Oh, they asked very inoffensive
questions about every one of the nine, except about our
own self.
"Lord in Heaven, have mercy upon us!"

Shortly thereafter, two were "invited" to come along for
interrogation during the midnight hours. Weeks later we
had to send their belongings to their parents ... they
would never return. Then one of the seven left, cracked
under the pressure. Rather than implicating others ... we
found him in his room, hanged. One of the six was missing
for days on end. We scoured the building; he was
discovered in the attic; he had chosen the same way out.
The fifth shot himself in the woods.
A couple of weeks later, nearing midnight, there was a
raucious knock at my door. Finding it unlocked, it was
opened and the light switched on.
"Heil, Hitler, the van is waiting, you are wanted for
interrogation."
I jabbered in tongues: "Lord, Jesus Christ, what am I
to do now?" My eyes fell on the camera: "Hmm," I heard
myself saying yawningly, "is it that they missed seeing me
at the meeting this evening? Is that the charge?"

I owe my life to Jesus--You also?

The guy in front turned to the two posted at attention at the door. They nodded their heads. I continued: "Why not take the camera and develop the film ... that ought to be plenty of proof that they overlooked me."

"Alright, take the camera ... we'll inform you in the morning about the outcome." They switched the light out, and closed the door.

That had been an uncomfortably close call. The speaker of the three was a friend. He played his role perfectly, for he knew exactly what the score was. The two at attention had not been initiated. All three, however, were commissioned, not acting on their own.

Two months later, I stood in the chow-line, bantering with fellow students, when a Nazi cordon (also students) entered, a group currying political favors to survive, and forge ahead. I knew one of them, for I had helped him with some problems, he was a loyal friend. Today he looked the other way, bumped into me hooking my leg, tripping me, he hugged me and whispered into my ears: "Get out, you're next, and no one can stop them." Then he took me and yelled at me what I thought of planting him a leg and tripping him. He threw me out of the line-up and he and his crowd took over my place. The commotion had drowned all else ... no one liked to tangle with that gang. No one blamed me for leaving.

I ran, packed my seven things and took the next train to Bonn. No one knew where I had gone ... my papers stayed where they were. My grandmother and Aunt Johanna informed my parents. As a woman I still had a way to extricate myself from the mess. The grapevine had it, that I had eloped. That ended my career as a physician. I signed up now as a student at an Industrial School of Art. No one questioned me about my other studies; I lived "at home" with my grandmother.

The Lord had done it again!

=82 =

35: The Lord's timing is perfect

ACTS 16, 9:
A vision appeared to Paul by night, the vision of a Macedonian standing and appealing to him with the words: "Cross over to Macedonia and help us!"

I had a similar vision by night, which also reminded me again of the vision I had on the Mountain of Our Lady. This time an American was standing on the other side of the ocean waving to me and saying, "come to the United States, we need you here."

A theologian, my mother was delighted, and how could I refuse ... we were officially engaged. He, too, was studying in Berlin at the time. Our courtship was something else ... kaleidoscopic, full of missed appointments, and strange chains of misunderstandings. He transferred to another university, from which he received his doctorate.

He was disappointed that I would not become his room mate for the duration. He left for the States and accepted a position. For a time I had thought no more of that pursuit. Now in a second vision the Lord reminded me of HIS will. In fact, the Lord prevented me from getting involved in his work in Bonn. Freight trains began rolling, leaving the West loaded with military hardware for the Eastern Front. Germany was getting ready for war.

The Lord dictated a letter to my lover: "Do you still want to marry me?" The answer was not long in waiting: "Of course, any day, if you can pay for the fare!"

I gathered a whole household and arranged for overseas transportation.

Meanwhile, my parents had decided to move to Darmstadt. Here my father had gone to High School. That is where his best friend and his brother lived. This was expedient, because his trips to the clinic in Frankfurt had become more frequent and lengthy. This was also out of reach for the henchmen who had tried so hard to apprehend him.

Here in the new house my household was set up.

Just before Easter 1939, I received Nazi clearance for

the shipment to the USA. This included also all the silver and other valuables from the Langenbachs not yet registered with the State. They hoped that at least one of their three children would survive. However, if none of them should live to claim it, I should feel happy about its ownership. (Thanks to the Lord, their oldest daughter survived and feels blessed by His providence.)

I had no way to determine on which freighter my goods were to be transported. It depended on the availability of space. It was scheduled to arrive in New Orleans either on August 15, or 18. It was in God's hands. Now my mother took her household out of storage and made herself at home in the new house. August seemed very far away, and I thought I would be in the USA long before that time.

In the ensuing 9 months I had three wedding ceremonies, and yet, like my confirmation, I do not remember any of them. Marrying was easy, but to obtain a passport was another matter. The war had begun in the East. By August they had discovered my medical training, and had me classified as **occupationally essential personnel.** That meant: **NO** passport.

I finally convinced an official that I had automatically lost my German citizenship by marrying a foreigner, a valid reason for issuing me a passport for stateless people. He agreed, and made out one of these and submitted it to the emigration bureau for validation. It was returned to him without processing. He decided against sending it in again. It was already the end of August. He had tried his best. What to do in this situation? At last he swayed his head weightily ... he resolutely pasted my picture in the proper space, he reached for a rubber stamp lying on his desk and affixed the imprint. He handed it to me to fill out the rest.

Then he put down his signature in such a way that it was impossible to decipher. He handed it to me wishing me God's speed: "Whatever its validity, that is the best I can do for you!" I shook his hand thankfully. At a glance I read the rubber stamp, it said: "Heil Hitler".

"Any way", I thought, "Lord, the whole thing was not my idea, if YOU want me in the United States, YOU will see me through."

I took leave of my parents, hired a taxi to take me and all my baggage to the railroad station for Rotterdam. At this date all German steam and freight lines had stopped running. The freighter to arrive in New Orleans on the 15th of August had accomplished its trip. The freighter to arrive on the 18th, however, was recalled on the high seas to return to home port lest they be confiscated as contraband. There was no telling where my household was!

The train was filled with American citizens fleeing Europe. At the border the train ground to a halt. Tickets or no tickets, everyone had to leave the train and the baggage was set out on the platform. It was mobilization day in the Netherlands. The regular border guards had been drafted, and their posts were filled by military personnel. The one confronting us spoke only Dutch and French. I translated what I could: "Do you have any tickets OUT of the Netherlands?"

Hesitatingly, the American pulled out a steamship ticket on a now cancelled German liner from his vest pocket. He slowly unfolded it, map-sized, and on both sides of it was sprawled in bold lettering **D O V E R.** I said emphatically "YES". He clapped into his hands, and a platoon of soldiers jumped to attention, "See to it that these people get to Rotterdam with their belongings."

Having nothing else to do to break the monotony of waiting around for a train, many hands picked up our baggage and stoved it away in a compartment on the train indicated.

No one was interested in my passport ... I was in the Netherlands, a stateless person, and beyond extradition. Praised be the Lord!

36: The Lord is faithful protecting you from harm

2 THESSALONIANS 3,3:
"However, the Lord is faithful; he will be sure to strengthen you and protect you from all harm."

Never before or after in the history of the Netherlands will there be a repetition of those three summer months, July, August, September including two weeks of October 1939. More than ten thousand Americans were stranded in Rotterdam waiting for a passage home. I added myself.

The Youth Hostel in Rotterdam had turned into a Grand Central Station, except with one reservation: The Youth Hostel Father enforced absolute curfew between 11 PM and 6 AM by turning off the main switch for the lights. I was an old hand at Youth-hosteling. My father had been one of the founders of the Youth Hostel Organization between 1902 and 1907. As his daughter, naturally, I held an international pass which entitled me to use hostels where I found them.

At the Youth Hostel in Rotterdam every bed was taken, and the pads, stored in slots by day, filled all available floor space during the night. No one complained about the accommodations, we thought them luxurious. Other Americans did not fare as well. Even people in fur coats slept on the piers for lack of money. The queue for cables home wound for blocks around the American Embassy. Three of the largest passenger ships lay in the harbor. Provisions for more than six thousand people were on board. The scheduled departures had been posted for September 18, 21, and 24. The Americans blew all their European money. The city had never before booked such lavish earnings; the Americans gave parties, bought clothing, books, keepsakes, plants and bulbs, you name it, figuring that European money will be useless if a war materialized. At departure time every last cent was spent. That is how they streamed to the pier.

At the pier they were confronted by the police telling them that the boats would not sail because the Dutch sailors had gone on strike. They demanded two way pay; because of the mines in the Channel they demanded additional insurance, and the company, fearing hard times to follow, did not want to do so. They knew they would return with empty ships. What was there to be done?

The Company decided to hire one way personnel except for the skeleton crew to sail back safely. Therefore, the Youth Hostel became the busiest training ground for waiters, stewards, window cleaners, kitchen help, recreation directors, barbers, hair dressers, nurses, and three complete bands. Every profession was aspired. These young people had been hired for a one way ticket.

Do you know what it takes to train three bands in 10 or 15 days? These Sunday and Monday musicians had been engaged for the trip, 60 or more guys and girls. Some of them had to go out and buy an instrument, they lacked music sheets, and had to decide on a repertory.

The Youth Hostel piano was taken apart, restrung and tuned. The ships had percussion instruments on board; as at present kitchen utensils had to substitute. The noise in the Youth Hostel was deafening ... only broken by the curfew. Where there is a will, there is a way! A week later when the strike was settled, each group was confident they could keep their fellow Americans entertained around the clock till they would reach the shore. They intoned: **A Mighty Fortress is Our God, a Trusty Shield and Weapon; HE helps us free from every Need that hath us now overtaken ...**

I had no chance on any of the passenger lines, because I had no reservation, no money, and no visa. The Netherlands were full of refugees. I reported to the consulate. I had to present myself for a physical. There women of all ages were lined up stark naked for hours on end awaiting their turn. I balked ... I had an up-to-date transcript from my physician. They took me in right away, and were satisfied with listening to my heart and lungs, and checking for V.D. My application for a visa as a U.S. bride was part of the next dispatch per cable to Washington.

After October 12, the hostel turned very quiet. I and several other students had found less expensive passages on a Norwegian freighter, a fast motor boat which expected to reach Panama via Boston within 10 days. It was a beautiful boat and I was loath to give it up. I did not receive my visa in time for sailing. A Mormon from Utah took my place ... it sailed during the wee hours. By afternoon someone called the hostel: "The freighter has struck a mine just four hours out of Rotterdam, and sank in minutes ... only those on deck could be saved."

The next day I received my visa.

I owe my life to Jesus--You also?

37: Be confident, I'll never fail you!

ACTS 27, 9; 22-23:
**"By this time it was far on in the season and sailing had
become dangerous ... I now bid you cheer up ... For
last night an angel of God ... stood by me, saying,
'Have no fear, Paul must stand before Caesar...'"**

A Liberty Freighter, the City of Joliette, was waiting for
clearance to sail. It was sitting on the water like a nut
shell, baring its hulk; a sad and bedraggled sight. The
captain refused cargo or ballast for fear of further delays;
British suspicion might accuse him of running contraband.
His fears were well grounded. Before the harbor of Dover
hundreds of ships were stranded waiting for clearance in
the "ship cemetary". This way, the decks were open and
anyone could convince himself at a glance that there were
no obstructions between the sky and the bare hull.

The captain had overbooked on passengers, he did not
want to split a family of six. The State Department was
cabled; at two o'clock in the morning he received the
permission to proceed.

The captain looked like a junk dealer; "What's the use to
shave, or dress up? Bah, the fishes don't care."

He was generous to his men. "Take all the free time you
desire ... Want your wages? Sure, I pay you out now.
Save the paint, let it peel!" The ship looked accordingly
... "Why exhaust the men with useless labor? If we strike a
mine, who cares in what condition the boat hits the bottom?
I want all my men on deck, well-rested, able to save
themselves."

His men loved him for it; they had pledged to refurbish
the ship inside and out, spic and span, before reaching
home berth, a promise which they kept.

That night at 2:30 A.M. the anchors were lifted. Our
Dutch friends below on the pier pitied us. However, even
they agreed, that it was better than not sailing at all. It
did not matter to me; I had my visa, and I was on board.
If the Lord had in mind to see me drowned, HE would have
left me on the Norwegian freighter. I never doubted that
we would reach the States without a mishap, if for no other
reason than that I was on board.

=89 =

I owe my life to Jesus--You also?

For the captain, a safe passage needed Divine intervention. His orders were to use the Northern shipping lane, traveling in the protection of military escorts. This aroused his ire. In front of all the passengers he gave the following dictation to his wireless operator:

"I refuse to take Northern shipping lane. The City of Joliette has no cargo or ballast. I am responsible for the safe passage of 18 passengers in addition to the crew.

The City of Joliette cannot make headway in winds of 25 to 35 mphs; in gusts of 65 mph the ship is bound to break up. At 10 mph headwind, the City of Joliette is only able to do 3 knots per hour. If the Company insists on the Northern route it must assume full liability for all lives on board. I am setting course for the Azores in order to reach the trade winds. With the current and tail wind we expect arrival in Houston within twenty days. End."

No one interfered. We huddled in the November wind, watching the sea gulls soaring and diving. Ships passed us. Days later the sky turned blue, and the air balmy. We lazied in the sun.

The wireless operator kept us informed. A sister ship with cargo obliged, taking the Northern Route. On the eighth day we were informed: "Bridge washed over board... 3 men lost!" Not for us ... the current and the trade winds pushed us with the speed of a bicycle at 18 knots per hour across a very smooth Atlantic Ocean.

At last we reached the land of **Freedom**, and of **PLENTY**. After 26 days at sea we again had solid ground under our feet. The Harbor of New Orleans is the backdoor to the United States of America. For this immigrant there was no welcoming committee. Our little party hired a truck for all eighteen people, two crew members, and the accumulation of baggage. The berth of the City of Joliette lay at the furthest possible point out in the harbor, miles away from the bus depot to New York, Detroit, Utah and California. By the time I had secured my ticket I had but 15 cents left. It did not matter, we had reached the great land.

38: For by hospitality some have entertained angels

Mark 7,6; 18-23; 7, 8:
"It was about you hypocrites indeed that Isaiah prophesied! ...nothing outside a man can defile him? It does not enter his heart ... it is what comes from the man that is what defiles him. From within, from the heart of man the designs of evil come..." -- "You drop what God commands and hold to human tradition."

New Orleans was the back door for new arrivals on American soil. The traces of the depression still lingered everywhere.
     The Land of Freedom and equality of opportunity was very much divided, indeed. For instance, there were two waiting rooms at the bus depot, one for Whites only, spacious, clean, with comfortable clean furnishings, plush easy chairs and love seats, while the other was half the size, with few wooden benches, overcrowded, dirty, grimy, with impossible toilet facilities outside.

Ours was a very long wait. According to the schedule, it would take twenty hours before our bus was due to pull into the station. As it was, the day at hand was still very young!
     My companion had the name of a Christian minister in New Orleans. Food from the ship was gone. Since we had nothing to do, we decided to hike six miles out to the luxurious parsonage. We found the pastor and his wife at home.
     "Ask and you will be given," truly, I had a language barrier ... yet I should not have traded my God for his God, but who was I to take the lead? The American was not free in Christ Jesus. He had never learned to ask. A rest was very much needed, but after one hour of small talk we were dismissed without refreshments, or food of any kind, and no place to turn. Under clear blue sky we walked the six miles back to town. A fierce wind was whistling in the tree tops ... the coldest day of the year,

the bananas froze on the stem. It was the 10th of December.

The visit gave me an inkling of what was to follow. Americans are too quick in attaching labels to their fellow men. They do not discriminate on individual merit. Once I was stamped an "enemy alien", I was stripped of all dignity and basic rights.

Tired and weary, we reached the inner city. Our feet ached, after all we had not had even a short walk in 26 days, much less accustomed to walking hard pavement non-stop for two hours. We were hailed from across the street ... a fellow traveler from our ship. He had been sulking; ever since the chess tournament two days ago. He thought he had it wrapped up and I had beat him. Now the Lord had changed his heart.

The Catholic priest invited us to help him while away his waiting time. The rave of New Orleans at the time were freshly baked donuts dipped in cinnamon sugar. He ordered a dozen. God bless his soul!
In a delightful manner he apologized for his embarrass- ment at losing a chess tournament to a female. To his knowledge, females were not known to have brains enough to succeed in chess. This was my introduction to the American way of classifying women below men. In the Germany I had just left, women were the greatest obstacle to the Nazis preventing them from wiping the church of Jesus Christ off the map. To my knowledge all mankind was equal before the Lord ... cowards or heroes, and the great majority just luke warm. This was a new twist, labeling women as inferior to men!

The bus was divided in half, that is, the larger front end of the bus was reserved for Whites, and the smaller back end for Blacks. The back was always crowded. The cruelest was that at some stops only part of the family was allowed to board for lack of space in the back part, while

I owe my life to Jesus--You also?

"white seats" went begging.

After a wearying trip I arrived safely in my new home. The freedom in Christ spared me many trials and tribulations brought on by those who rather disregarded God's commandments to preserve human traditions. I was innocent, and never innitiated. My husband, I should discover in retrospect, was hooked on drugs. Inevitably he had used up his mother's small inheritance. He was persona non grata at home. His family had been in no mood to extend further aid in helping him to set up housekeeping ... I had no inkling of any problems. When his father perceived my genuine innocence, he was persuaded by his love for me and his deep respect for anything German, to forgive his son. We both were accepted into the family.

I was conscious of the barrier between myself and my husband, and the barrier between us and his family. They never involved me in anything. God spared me the agony of knowing the reason. The Lord was leading me in HIS way ... strange and wonderful ... HE thought of everything.

Now you would like to know what had become of my household shipment? Of course, the Lord took care of that also! It had arrived on the last German freighter to unload in the United States. It was on schedule, waiting for me in New Orleans since the 15th of August. It was again Easter time, exactly one year later when it arrived in excellent condition all in one box on top of a large truck. Now I had everything to set up housekeeping.

The Lord does all thing well ... have courage, oh my soul, and forget not that HE is with you. I had hoped that my God was to become his God. I knew that my prayers would find favor before HIM. As HE had guided me in Germany, Jesus Christ would guide me here, too.

HE remains the same for ever.

39: Jesus talks to ordinary people like you and me
MARK 4, 9-24:

"Anyone who has ears to hear, let him listen to this ... these are the people who listen to the word and take it in ... Nothing is hidden except to be disclosed, nothing is concealed except to be revealed ... Take care what you hear; the measure you deal out to others will be dealt out to yourselves, and you will receive extra."

There is only ONE GOD, and only ONE JESUS CHRIST. HIS WORD is the same for all mankind, ask any foreigner, he will tell you this is true; and there are over five hundred languages around the world. GOD'S WORD is the same and his translation is called the Bible. Human words go in and out of fashion, GOD'S WORD remains the same. Therefore it is important that we refrain from worshipping human words.

For example, if one wishes to read Shakespeare in the original, it is appropriate to use a special dictionary ... but to enjoy a play on the stage one needs to hear it in the language our ears are accustomed to. In like measure, the Churches and the Sunday Schools should not be used to give free lessons in the 16th century language in an attempt to show the meaning of the WORD of GOD. This is regrettable, especially when the lessons are given by well meaning, but poorly informed instructors. It is a matter of worshipping tradition, or of understanding GOD'S WORD. I, as all foreigners, do not share a tradition in the printed language; neither do the youngsters, they have trouble reading as it is. I liked to use my Bible, because the LORD spoke to me as if my own father.

There is no such thing as an authentic printed edition of GOD'S WORD. When Christ walked the earth printing had not yet been invented. Christ spoke, and the disciples remembered and retold HIS WORDS many, many times before they were committed to parchment. If not written down in Aramaic, the language Christ used, then the first written document was in Greek, right away translated into a different language. The Catholic Church uses the Vulgata, that is, ordinary Latin, "Street Latin", so that the ordinary, uneducated people should understand its content. It, too, is abbridged and censored. As such it has become a venerable document, and a sacred tradition. Some of the new editions of modern Bibles are also "abbridged" (simplified and shortened), and "edited" ... look at the frontis page of your Bible, verify and make certain that it is a true **translation.** If it is, you cannot go wrong.

God speaks to us through human interpretation, the human language, that is, the language we are most familiar with. Let me illustrate what I mean.

Imagine you are facing a Vietnamese villager and you tell him in English: "I have a permanent home for you, clothing, and food enough for the rest of your days, because I love you." You wait ... no reaction, nothing happens. Now the translator translates what you have said in his dialect. Now his arms will fall around your neck and the man has happiness written all over him. THIS IS WHY OUR FATHER IN HEAVEN wishes to talk to us in a language we can readily understand. Pictures, ornaments, and antiques are nice, but for true appreciation one must first study the period taking art lessons. OUR FATHER IN HEAVEN does not want it to be that complicated.

We all take possession of a loved one and take him for granted: a child his mother, for example. Then you love her, you honor her, and revere her. When she is gone you grieve, you feel her loss, even if she has just gone around the corner.

Such is the wisdom of the Lord. His language is very plain. He does not wish to confuse us, to raise doubt, nor make us fear pitfalls.

PSALM 23, 3:

"HE guides me by true paths, as HE himself is true."

HIS WORD is meant for every ear, not just for an elected few. We must not worship and trust the elected few, or something which is incomprehensible, numinous and holy. GOD has no intentions to hide anything from us. Christ spoke the ordinary language of his day. Now HE speaks in ours. Therefore, let us broadcast the WORD as best as we can. He is OUR FATHER who speaks to HIS children, and HIS children have no problems in understanding their father. GOD and CHRIST expect us to understand THEIR WORD, likewise! Hallelujah, Amen!

40: Now don't drop that confidence of yours

LUKE 11, 42:

"...But woe to you! You tithe incense, horror, and repentence (rue), and every bit of food, but justice and the love of God you disregard: these latter you ought to have practiced--without omitting the former."

There was no thought of peace during the Christmas Season of 1942 ... hatred ran high even among ardent Christian people. Once there was a bake sale and an auction at the Mount Airy Church, which we had joined. I had baked a cake, but then the auction was over and my cake had disappeared. Therefore I asked the chairman: "What happened to the cake I had made?"

The lovely lady, the pillar of the Women's Guild, pulled my cake out from under the desk, lifted it up to the few still standing around: "Oh, yes, here is still that cake from **THAT GERMAN WOMAN**, who'd want that one?"

Some one said: "I'll take it for 36 cents".

"Sold", cried the chairman delighted, "and good riddance for a noble cause!"

At a regional church conference I did not fare much better. At best, I was tolerated to tag along. They were older by twenty or more years. Mrs. Ryne and Mrs. Rease were discussing sickness in the family, and were sighing, unable to solve the problem. I thought of some comforting words and prayers, when Mrs. Ryne turned to me and said: "Of course, you don't have children, and you have never dealt with sicknesses, you are much too young to understand our problems and concerns. Just wait until you are our age, then you can talk our language."

Truly, I was alone among men. Try as I may, I was given no chance to become a part of the community. Then the Mount Airy neighborhood association created an air-raid shelter! Everyone was invited for its dedication; of course we went. Refreshments, plentiful for all! Faces were beaming. Cornered, I was quite officiously asked: "How does this air-raid shelter compare with those in Europe?" I was stunned. I looked at the bare-rafter ceiling of the cellar. I looked at the miles of garden hose. I thought of the inadequate water pressure due to corroded pipes of the whole neighborhood. I looked at the array of buckets, and I thought: These poor people just don't have a concept of what 'war' really means. This, in Holland, Belgium, France and Germany would have been considered a tinder box, but not an air-raid shelter."
I hated to hurt the well-meaning people. I tried to suppress my urge to burst into laughter. And the longer I hesitated, the more intent the people strained to hear my answer. I took a deep breath, and at last said: "It is a lucky thing, that submarines (which were to have harassed the Jersey Coast just then) cannot fly!" It was an honest statement. It was not meant to hurt them, and it did not make me a liar.

Well, this quip would cause me nearly four years of serious trouble. You see, I was an enemy alien. "Could I have secret data, that perhaps, submarines really were meant to fly? From that day on I was under tight surveilance by the F.B.I. They never told me why they were interrogating me. What did they wished to know? Once, sometimes twice a week I had to make a pilgrimage to down-town Philadelphia (at my own expense) and visit my henchmen. The Gestapo could not have out-done them short of shortening my neck. Each interrogation lasted between two and four hours. Each time there was a court steno-typist present. She only took down my deposition without any questions. At the end of each six months, twice a year, they presented me with the accumulated, typed product, and told me: "Lift up your right hand and swear that these are your statements, made voluntarily, and uncoerced!"

"Where are your questions, to which I was required to answer? Without those pointed questions, I would never have given you this information." I refused.

I brought my husband along to argue the point in good English. Each time they dropped that request, but kept pounding out more and more questions. The stacks grew. I got a respite, having my baby and recuperating. We had moved out into the country. I needed F.B.I. permission to drive there and permission to visit the city. One time I wished to celebrate my birthday in Philadelphia, and I let the F.B.I. know of my intentions. They sent me a postal card saying: "If you come to Philadelphia on September 24, please stop at the office by two o'clock in the afternoon."

I had more enjoyable things to do on my birthday. Forget about that trip! But I kept the card, I assure you. At the end of October I received a subpoena from the Court. I took my card along, just to be safe. I wound my way through the halls of the new Court building, and was before the specified door at the appointed hour.

The judge sat in a rather dark room against the light from the window. He was writing. He laid down his pen. He checked my subpoena against the paper on his desk and then started upbraiding me for not heeding a summons from the F.B.I. I did not say as much as a word. I took my postal card out of my pocket, laid it into his hand and stepped back. He read it, taking more time then it required. He got hot under the collar. He jumped up, upsetting his chair, brushing past me in giant steps, literally running into the hall, and shouting: "Mr. the

F.B.I, you @#&*@#*@, how dare you? How dare you? Where are you?"

I followed to the doorway, to see what took place (inconspicuously), two agents, my two gents, came running. "Did you write this?" They looked at their card. The judge did not wait: "Based on this evidence, how dare you bother the Court, prevailing until a subpoena is issued. What right do you have to give orders to the Court?" The halls reverberated and echoed his words.

He turned and walked back to me, returning the card. He stretched out his hand and took mine, he patted me on the shoulder, and said softly: "Had I been you, I would not have come on that card, either. You have done right."

This nonsense came to an uprupt end in January 1946. All U.S. citizens were locked out. The press was locked out. They screened 500 immigrants, checking passports, I.D.s, birth certificates and finger prints. We filed past, and were told that none of us could leave the building until the last was processed. That was 8 o'clock in the morning. Guards and chaperones attended the inner doors, and the police shut out the public from the building.

At 8.30 A.M. the judge took his seat. We were sworn in as a group. The judge rapped his gavel, and announced the agenda for the day: **"The Court versus the F.B.I."** Then he added: "Mr. the F.B.I., any of the cases you have processed will be heard in full by this Court. Any case you cannot make stick, that person will be granted full citizenship ... Mr. the F.B.I., please begin: A... place the file before our Judgeship. Today your opportunity has come to convince the Court! We have a long way to go, don't waste time." He lifted up his face and viewed the audience.

Alphabetically, and one by one we were called into the witness stand. Name, address, sworn in, to tell the truth and nothing but the truth! So help me God ... Then the Judge asked benignly: "Mister, the F.B.I., name the charges to the Court". . . "Mister, the F.B.I., the Court wishes to know the charges, not hear-say! ... How long have you worked on this case? ... Four Years?"

It was five in the afternoon. "The F.B.I." was a crew of 10 or 12 men busily bringing piles upon piles of processed files into the court room on dollies; one or two changing off, taking the stand. We had arrived at the Wi..., and I was in the witness stand. The dolly was brought in with my files, four double columns hip-high. The Judge was livid: "Miiiister the AF.BEE.IIIYE, the Court wiiishes to know the charrrges! ... Four years ought to be enough time to know what the charges are ... Don't tell the Court, reeeeead the charges, rreeead what you have in your hand!"

One of my two F.B.I. men stood there, seemingly rattled. His hands were shaking, and he had trouble reading the paper: "On or about August 12, 1942, at the dedication of an air-raid shelter, the defendent made the following statement: **"It is a lucky thing that submarines can't fly!"** he fell silent.

"Quite true," said the judge dryly, "go on!" Silence. All of a sudden, gavel in hand, the judge flew out of his chair, down and in front of the two piles on the dolly ... the other F.B.I. man ducked, dropping the handle bar. The gavel threatened to fly off into his direction. The left hand stroked downward on each pile ... the judge's voice filled the hall livid with rage: "And, Miiiiister, the F.B.I., and what is thiiis?"--

It came a little over-loud: "These are the records of our investigation."

The judge roared: "The in-ves-ti-gaaaa-tion of what? Explain, Mister, the F.BEEE.EYE. --YOU HAVE THE FLOOR!"

No sound. The audience held its breath.

"Nothing; haaah; is that what gives you the license to proscribe guide lines to the Court? Was that perhaps the reason for demanding subpoenas from the Court?" Again unbroken silence. "Answer the Court: Have you, in all those four years, confronted the witness with the charges?" The gavel threatened the F.B.I. man who had the floor. He ducked, and the judge crouched to his level and snarled through his teeth: "Answer the Court, you MISTER, THE Fff. BBBe.III."

"No".

"The Court did not hear!" a black-winged sleeve flew up to the ear.

"No", a little firmer.

"Another question, Miiister the F.BEE.EYE: Have you confronted the witness with the plaintiff? Answer, MI-I-I-I-I-sters, the EEF.BEEE.EYE. the Court is waiting, that was not loud enough nobody could hear your answer, least of all the Court!" The Judge had returned to his seat. What followed next, cannot be decribed. The Judge, agile like a Tiger, flew down the steps. The F.B.I. man, horrified, backed against the dolly, the dolly with my files gave way and the agent went down backwards. The Judge booted in his direction: "Yes", roared the Judge, "take it along, take it along, and dare charge the Court for storage!"

The agent picked himself off the floor as fast as he could. He grabbed the handle of the dolly and hurried out of the door. The Judge hurried after him his robe flying behind him. He grabbed the door, opening it wide and shouted: "Get ready for the next case!" and let go of the door.

The judge wiped the sweat from his eye brows. He slowly climbed up the steps to his chair on level with mine. He looked over the assembly of the five hundred. Our cheek bones ached from suppressing the laughter, faces were tear stained, and handkerchiefs were wringing wet. The hall was fully alive with twittering noises, never loud, always contained, noses blowing, suppressed hiccups, and the like. The the Judge turned to face me fully: "Place your left hand on the Bible, lift up your right ... nothing but the truth. You hear! ... Nothing but the truth. Have

=101=

you ever made the statement" ... he interrupted himself, turning to the clerk: "Did you catch the charge?"

She read it to him. He repeated: ... "It is a lucky thing that submarines can't fly ... Now, nothing but the truth! You are under no pressure, and it really does not matter to the Court if you do not remember the incident!"

It was hard to keep a straight face, I said: "I do remember ... that is exactly what, and how I said it."

The Judge brought his gavel down hard, and shouted into the assembly: "The Court agrees with the defendant. The Court found Mister, the F.B.I. guilty for misusing the resources and the facilities of the Court." Again he turned to me; he shook my hand and, shielding his mouth from the ears of the recording clerk, said in an audible whisper: "Now, you must remember that you are in the **free** United States, but you have to think twice before talking over the fence, lest an F.B.I. agent should be listening in! Congratulations! God speed!"

X, Y, and Z, the end of a tantalizing day was reached. The F.B.I. was denounced in a twenty minute harrangue, and sentenced. Then all of us 500 witnesses in the hall received our citizenship papers. We were taken by limousines to the mansion of the Daughters of the American Revolution, invited to a grand banquet. We were seated at small tables, chaperoned by an attentive hostess. We had been sealed off from the world from eight in the morning until our dismissal shortly after seven in the evening. This was the end of my being an enemy alien, one year after the end of the actual war. This witch hunt had continued to run its course unabated on this side of the Atlantic. It brought no benefit of any kind to any one. The cost to the tax payers was enormous. The nightmare had ended.

PSALM 22, 23-36: "Praise the Eternal ... glorify him ... For he has not despised the poor man's plight, he has not hidden his face from me, he answered my appeal for help ... Let the pious partake of the feast, to their heart's desire ... wishing me LONG LIFE AND HAPPINESS!"

41: Set your heart on higher talents

1 JOHN 4, 18-20:
"Love has no dread in it; in deed, love in its fulness drives all fear away, for dread has to do with punishment ... We love, because HE loved us first. If anyone declares: "I love God, and hates his brother, he is a liar; for he who will not love his brother whom he has seen, cannot possibly love the God whom he has never seen ... He who loves God is to love his brother also."

I had gone to college to fill out my time ... my husband was sullen most of the time, unless on business, or with visitors. He spent much of his free time locked in his study, shunning bright light. Then he put in a ten hour day out of the house as an editor. I learned how to run business machines and located myself a job to augment "our insufficient" budget, turning it over to my husband trustingly. I was truly alone among men ... with the entry into the war, mail service from home was permanently disrupted. Hatred ran high during the Christmas Season of 1942 and my loneliness had become a burden. My job kept me occupied, but the mainstream of people were hostile to enemy aliens. Holidays were hard on me, partly because my husband had an aversion to them, and partly, because our celebrations at home had been so sincere and happy (a tribute also to my dear mother), that nothing could be a credible substitute in this country. Most of the preachers, and churches in general, don't know how to express happiness in Christ having become a man. Partly, they are afraid of people being truly happy, and partly, because the American dream of happiness involves sqandering resources, spending money, and indulging in excesses. Therefore, Christmas is turned into a John the Baptist Crusade, and a preparation for Good Friday, on the one hand, and on the other trivia, an entertainment for the kids like showing the movie "THE LITTLEST STAR" at a candle light service at

I owe my life to Jesus--You also?

11 P.M. on Christmas Eve. At home Christmas and Easter were sacred periods not even interfered with by the Nazis. In a way, New Year, also, was sacred.

New Year's Eve 1942/3 was no exception. I went to sleep in the Lord, as always. And while I was asleep, the Lord appeared to me and said: "I will fill your heart with gladness, and wipe out your loneliness." Then HE led me to a car; HE took me to see a farm with a bed of big white Easter lilies almost shoulder high, "this shall be yours, and then you shall have a baby boy." With that HE left, and I awakened. What a dream! A car, a farm and a ...? A car and a farm ... that was foolishness, we were always broke. That was a fancy at best. But to go overboard to believe that I could have a baby! With my medical history? How could I be sure I still had all the parts necessary? Had not most of my insides rotted and been removed at one time or other? Had they not shortened my intestines by a yard or so? So much for the dream. Besides, I had proof very soon that I was everything but pregnant.

We had a friend who was a Real Estate broker. He called us one day in January and invited us to come along to the Pennsylvania Dutch country to inspect 5 farms he had newly listed. It was a nice Saturday, but a cold outing. I loved the countryside for it reminded me of home. The farmers were fun to talk to, unpretentious. They did not care about labels ... German? So what! They were Germans, too, and even though somewhat removed by several generations, still spoke their home dialect. I loved especially one farm, but truly none of them matched the one in the dream ... the Lord had shown it to me in season. But I did not even stop to think; it was of no merit.

That Sunday we met at church; we talked about the lovely outing, and about the nice farm we saw. Someone jested: "Why not buy one?"

We laughed and said: "No, no, no, out of the question, we have no money, not any amount." Truly, it was not said regretfully, or with hidden regretfulness in either of us ... it was just something to talk and laugh about. But

at my elbow, turned away, stood a little old lady, hardly 5
feet tall. She tapped me on the sleeve and said:

"If you would like to have the farm, I can lend you the
money. I'll be glad to invest what I have inherited from my
Lady, I trust you. I have a place in a nursing home paid
for life, and if you will pay me 3% in regular monthy
installments, I can let you have the whole amount."

During the next week I pawned my camera to be able to
buy a car, so we could drive out to take possession of our
farm. It needed a lot of fixing, and I still had my job in
town. On Easter my husband was out of town on business,
and I sat alone in the pew immersed in prayers for my
loved ones, for all those suffering in the war, old friends
and new friends. I asked the Lord for peace. Instead, the
Lord touched me: "Remember what I told you earlier?" I
turned hot and cold, I put my hands on my heart: "Lord,
such a promise is too much to hope for, you will have the
burden of seeing me through!" But then it became very
calm within me ... "if YOU, LORD, will it, be it thus" ...
I knew, I should truly have a baby!

By May the Easter lilies on the farm began sprouting,
they grew tall, and taller, until the huge blossoms opened
up in all their splendor. Now at last, I recognized that this
was the place the LORD had shown me in my vision ... The
biggest miracle was taking place within me. The LORD had
announced it, and now it filled me with warmth, courage
and hope. In June I was certain, and quit my job. I moved
to the farm for the rest of the season; I felt wonderful!

42: Blessed among women are you

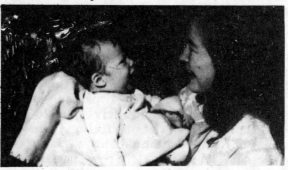

PSALM 103, 1-5:

"Bless the Eternal, O my soul, let all my being bless his sacred name ... remember all his benefits ... and all your sicknesses he heals, he saves your life from death, he crowns you with his love and pity, he gives you all your heart's desire, renewing your youth like an eagle's."

The Lord knew that I needed to be needed. This little life the LORD had entrusted to me was melting away every anxiety or selfish thoughts I may have harbored. This blessed miracle ... even through the bleakest winter I never faltered in the knowledge that I should be victorious. Blunders and tribulations ... yet HE brought me through unscathed as HE had promised. When my little one strained to get on his feet, and the Easter lilies began to sprout, I was back on the farm.

This ushered in the happiest time of my life. The Lord made me feel younger than I had ever been at any time during my teens. He held away all the clouds from this lovely piece of ground, and left it untouched by the war. The barn yard provided us with fowl, the garden with vegetables and fruit, the fields with corn, hay and wheat. The farmers loved and accepted me and my baby, and we loved every one of them. Winter came much too soon, and we had to return to the city, for the farm was not winterized.

43: Teach the very young the love of Jesus

JOB 33, 15-16:
>"In dreams, in visions of the night, when men fall into trances, slumbering on their beds, he reveals things to them, and sends them awful warnings, to draw them back from evil, and make them give up pride, to save their souls from death, their lives from rushing on to doom."

Amid all this rejoicing, bustling and happiness in January 1945, I had another vision. In this dream the Lord showed me this one year old child grown to a man of twenty one. I was on the Express Way which was not yet conceived on the drafting board. I saw the sky line of Philadelphia bathed in golden sunshine, a skyline which did not yet exist; yet I could pick out the Museum and William Penn on top of City Hall. Then there was a crash; it grew dark. I was stranded on the Express Way. In deepest night this son of mine came to my rescue. His father was no more, I stood alone, but he himself was independent also.

Twenty years is a long time span. It was unthinkable that something could happen to the three of us. Life is for the living; the dream, however startling and etched into my mind, did not unduly alarm me. It reminded me of the treasures the Lord had heaped upon me, and encouraged me **"to make the very most of my time."** (Col.4, 6) It reminded me that our life is precious. But it did not serve as a warning that I had a duty to instill into the heart of the child a fear of God, and a belief that Jesus Christ lived also for him. I thought that was an automatic prerogative of the theologian, his father. I should have known better, for he never prayed, he read prayers, mostly the same, he did it because it was expected of him. The name of Jesus was seldom mentioned. He despised himself, and had dreadful nightmares. Weekends and holidays were spoiled by his father having drug-withdrawal problems.

All this did not touch me. I was with the child, I praised God's grace in song, in the spirit, and in tongues. As before, wherever I walked, Jesus went, too. In my own house I remained an enemy alien, laughed at, good for nothing, and despised.

I am guilty, I did not heed the warning. I did not take the lead in spiritual matters, I did not teach my baby to walk with Christ. Going to church and being baptized was not enough. That was the domain of his father's trade. I am guilty ... his mother was all that counted in his life until he became a man; then he found nothing to lean on ... no faith in Jesus Christ. How can a woman set an example for a son to become a man? Now I can only pray that the Lord will bless that small seed I tried to put into his heart; that it will germinate and blossom into genuine love for the Lord.

Just because I was never asked about my faith, I was too shy to volunteer to talk about it. Neither did I have the chance to meet others who felt likewise. In Germany Christians endangered their lives if they talked openly about their faith. Each one for himself ... the reason why the Nazis could deal so harshly with the individual. Here you have blossoming congregations, and no faith to talk about.

At the time, however, I was very unconcerned about what would happen in twenty years. I loved every minute of my new-found love, convinced that the Lord would help me step by step to do the right thing.

I owe my life to Jesus--You also?

44: Jesus gave his disciples the power of healing

MATTHEW 10, 1:
And summoning his twelve disciples he gave them power over unclean spirits, power to cast them out and also to heal every sickness and disease.

We were hard up. The previous winter had been a financial drain with me and the baby in the hospital for three weeks, and then getting very slowly on my feet. But now I was fine and the baby had ne'er a complaint. Jesus reminded me that I had the skills of healing, and that there was a great need, a nurses shortage on the home front.

I contacted local pediatricians to let them know about my speciality in giving premature babies, and others with problems, a start in life. Soon, my little one and I made the rounds through a number of households.

With the Lord's help, I picked up from the hospital one hapless bundle after another, at 3 1/2 pounds, 4 or 5 pounds, or a baby weighed in at birth with 8 lb. and down to five. Each time the pediatrician was certain that, left in the hospital, the baby was sure to die. I improvised incubators, dumped 5 or more formulas inside of 48 hours, until we got the little thing to respond. Then my baby and I moved on to pick up the next one. I loved it, and thrived on the happiness I was able to give to the mother and the whole family.

I knew what my calling should have been. I could have had a license for practical nursing for the asking ... it was then not a stringent requirement. No one pointed out to me that it might come in handy at a future date. As it was, the two of us were most welcome and much appreciated. We did not have to part from each other, day or night.

=109=

45: Jesus is faithful, remembering his promises
ISAIAH 42, 6-9:

> "I the Eternal have called you of set purpose, I have taken you by the hand, I have formed you for the rescuing of my people, for a light to nations ... to free captives from their bondage, darkened lives from prison. I am the Eternal, the true God: ...My former predictions have now come to pass..."

My former vision on the Mountain of our Lady had come to pass. The infamous war had ended, neither the God-fearing nor the evil fared well. Every inch of my native land was fought over, the devil received a new name, that is, "German". Darmstadt, the city my father and mother had chosen for their new residence, was one among 60 large cities of over 100,000 inhabitants, sheet-bombed. In the conflagration 56,000 civilians lost their lives in one single night. Yet, at no time did it occur to me to doubt that I would see them again. Perhaps I thought at times that it was preposterous to expect my father to be still among the living, just to consider the advanced cancer on his hip. But then, the Lord had promised it. The "how", in this case too, was in HIS hands.

The war had ended, and I received a military depot letter, from an officer from Utah. I opened it on the spot: "Your parents' house, at the eastern edge of the town, is one of seven houses still standing. We have made this house military headquarters, off limits to the men. Will is in his bedroom, and Mart is chief in the kitchen ... they are waiting for kitchen supplies, since Darmstadt has not seen a food shipment in a year. Will at 5' 11", is weighing in with 126 lb., and Mart at 5', with 85 lb. All of us are cheerful and well. We are not permitted to fraternize with the Germans. I hope you will write me."
Praise the Lord, my father and my mother were well in their own house and in good hands!

As if that had not been enough good tidings to receive in one day! Oh, no, there was another letter, bedraggled quite forbidding from the British Command Headquarters from Birmingham, England. I even let it wait until the chores were done. Lo' and behold, it was a letter from my brother:

"Dear Sister, I am well, a war prisoner. One day heavy fog settled over Belgium; my comrade and I were to repair the telephone line. Holding onto the line we followed it out of headquarters. A bomb wiped out the headquarters behind us. The fog dragged on for days. We were starved, wet, and dog-tired. We had lost all sense of directions, when we were stopped by a Britsh Commando. Without food we were stuck into a cellar with an iron grill in a passage way. Days went by; we were forgotten. Then I heard a voice overhead, a voice of a pal of mine. I shouted my name, and he recognized mine. That was my salvation. From then on I was with the others. Your brother."

I wept tears of joy. Right away I sat down and wrote to the G.I. from Utah, that my brother was alive, that they were grandparents, and all of us well. That done, I penned five letters to my brother, with basically the same information: that our parents were alive, and the house still standing. All six letters were supplied with three snapshots of us three. I was confident that at least one letter would make it, to my brother. By God's grace one of them did!

This is what he told me much later: "Your letter was the only link with the outside which penetrated our prison camp for the duration of five full months. This letter went through all hands time and again; your handwriting had faded, even the last traces had been kissed away. Your words were inscribed in every heart.

"We were permitted to write a restricted number of letters and cards. To my knowledge yours was the only one which reached its destination. No one ever will comprehend what your letter meant to all of us!"

Such happiness ... only the Lord could have arranged that those two letters met in my mailbox on the same day!

46: What you do to the least of them, do it unto me

GALATIANS 6, 9-10:
"... never let us grow tired of doing what is right, for if we do not faint we shall reap our harvest at the opportune season. So then, as we have opportunity, let us do good to all men and in particular to the household of the faith."

The infamous and cruel war had ended; the underground had not received a helping hand. The need among those who had fought since 1936 was immense. I had given many names of these to the Red Cross, but only 40% could be located alive. One by one they were sent back to me with new addresses. Attached to these names were brief profiles. One of those read: "Hanna Dibelius; Present Loc.: Hamburg; Facil.: 2 rooms, bombed out shell, cellar, damp, open; Dependents: 2 ,age 4 & 7, tall; Remarks: pregn. 7th m., husband, returned Russ. prisoner of war, dying in Berlin. Special Need: survival ration. On Hand: 0." The date was November.

A down-town church had set up a request pool, and baling center, into which I entered what could not be taken care of otherwise. Bless these generous souls who took it upon themselves to aid these hapless. This is what happened: The good soul who pulled Hanna's name made haste. She gathered a layette for the unborn, good used clothing for the mother and the two children, blankets for all four, a sterno stove, oatmeal, sugar, lard, a formula, and other staples. It was baled and sped on its way.

Ten years later this is what Hanna told me through

tears: "I was asked to claim a package. I was unable to carry it, and they helped me. Before we reached the door of our abode I started in final labor and collapsed. They put me on the bare floor where I gave birth to the baby. We had nothing, no heat, no food; nothing to put on the baby and nothing to replace the wet rags on me. When I could breathe again there was this bale. Someone cut it open. The children sat wide-eyed and in stupor. I must have fainted. When I came to, the women ran with a pail of water, there was soap, washcloths, and towels. I was washed ... my rags were dumped. I was completely dressed with ski pants and coat, wrapped into the blanket. The baby was washed and dressed and swaddled. The older ones were treated in turn the same way. Meanwhile, the sterno was put to work and we got the first hot meal in months. I cried myself to sleep with an overwhelmingly thankful heart, praising the Lord for this providence. It was the greatest miracle that God had remembered my name! How that this lady could know my needs and had packed the correct sizes? We still correspond."

The Lord works his miracles, his timing was perfect. The Red Cross received my request, and found her. I lost no time, and the ladies acted; the package was dispatched; at arrival Hanna was located. From the beginning to the end, such synchronization could not have been arranged by humans! The kindness and love these hapless had shown to others before, came back to them in even larger measure in their hour of need--those **(2 Cor. 8, 1-15) who had little had not too little** to be generous with time and gifts. During this crisis, all my earnings went into endless relief packages. I and many, many others, spared no effort to help. It filled us with warmth, and thankfulness to a generous measure ... none of us should lack anything, and found still more to give. No obstacles were too great to overcome.

Praise the Lord for his mercy, love and compassion!

47: Your faith has saved you

PSALM 5, 1-3:
"O thou Eternal, listen to my words, and hear the murmur of my soul; my King and God, give ear to my appeal, for I am calling out to thee; oh, hear my morning prayer, for in the morning I set forth my plea, waiting Thine answer."

Living on the farm entailed driving my husband to the commuter train, a trip of a good half hour. In good weather this was no problem, but in bad weather? One day we had dense fog, and I decided to leave the baby where he was, sound asleep in the playpen, covered up warmly and safe. I drove through the fog. Just before the railroad station I saw the train pulling in very slowly into the station, and my husband hurried from the car into the train and it continued its trip.

I just had reached the car and opened the door when the Lord's voice commanded me to go into the waiting room and wait. I slammed the door and went into the waiting room. Here I seated myself on a bench with no thoughts whatever, but watching the hand of the clock jerk from minute to minute ... "5 minutes, 6 minutes, 7 minutes.." I got up and said out loud: "Lord, this is ridiculous, YOU know my baby is at home alone, and I still have another 45 minutes to drive through this pea soup of YOUR making, and to boot, it's getting thicker by the minute. I cannot delay the return trip any longer."

Resolutely I got into the car and entered the six lane highway on the first leg for home. Truly, all I could see was the inside white stripe, demarking the bounds of the center strip. I zipped down the lane at about 25 miles an hour, the window open, wipers going. Suddenly I heard brakes ahead and slowed down. Then I saw the red lights in front of me. We still rolled a ways, and then we stood for good. The cars behind me did the same. None of us could see the cause or reason for the stoppage. So we lost no time; we left our cars, and walked ahead. What a terrible mess! All we saw was wreckage of cars, a trailer truck, a dump truck, goods, bodies, people groaning and moaning. No police, no flares, goods, trash, strewn everywhere across all six lanes and in the fields. Most of it wrapped into a veil by the fog. We came to the eighth car still standing, just accordionized front and back, its owner had opened the door and climbed out dazed. I asked him: "But, when did this happen?"

With shaking hands the man pulled a watch on a chain from his pocket; opening the lid he said: "Just about seven minutes ago."

48: Never cease to give thanks

ACTS 14, 17

"...though as the bountiful Giver he did not leave himself without a witness, giving you rain from heaven and fruitful seasons, giving you food and joy to your heart's content."

Living on the farm was by design of the Lord ... the war was far away, and the strife of the city did not touch the land. The city cannot exist without the good will of the land, and the farmer cannot exist without the goodwill of the Lord. The Bible speaks about the shepherd; in this day and age Jesus Christ would have spoken of the farmer. His job begins at the crack of dawn and ends after sundown, and often not even then. By farmer I do not mean just the man, no indeed, by "farmer" I mean man, wife and child, and every one living on a farm. Their day cannot be limited to punch cards as practiced behind the Iron Curtain; neither can he fight for overtime pay: the owner of the farm, like the shepherd, is God's helper. If need be, he will get up in the middle of the night, a flashlight in hand, disregarding rain and sleet. If need be, he will take a rope, tie it to his tractor, drive it to the meadow to a cow in labor. He talks to the animal comfortingly, ties the rope to the hindfeet of the protruding calf, gets back on his tractor and pulls ever so gently, until it is born. A hired hand does not take that responsibility.

That is the reason why the communists cannot make out. The land has been disowned, the farmers dispersed; the second generation already knows no better, they are hired hands, wage earners. Cattle, cows, in particular, are state-owned, their milk is government milk. Crops, like beans, peas and potatoes, are state-responsibility, so are fowl, and eggs.

"The State" means no one in particular ... like the Nazis, "the STATE" has no face, I have never met one ... an "organization" has no need for God. To the contrary, an organization is jealous of God, it tries to alienate people from the Lord. Jesus Christ is walking with each of us on a one to one basis.

I owe my life to Jesus--You also?

I lived on the farm. The place the Lord had selected for me lay in the midst of lovely neighbors, the Boyers, the Fegelys, the Welders, the Eckarts, Glicks and the Masts, to mention a few. Believe me, as a city girl that I was, I needed plenty of teachers and I worked on my lessons. Just to let you have a taste of what they were up against:

I purchased a Sears incubator and put into it hen eggs, two duck eggs, and two goose eggs and expected a successful hatch ... To tell you the truth, I did not fare too badly, I raised 24 chicks, one duckling and one gosling. The ones mixed up were the gander and the duck. This uneven pair shared everything: the feed, the stream ... Well, my neighbors kept an eye on it. In due time each one received a mate, and I put away the incubator, letting God take care of my fowl.

That spring season was very dry and everything depended on a good hay crop, and letting the seeds germinate in the fields. The farmers looked at the blue sky and shook their heads: "At this rate we will not have a crop this year."

I beseeched the Lord for rain, and during the afternoon one white cloud sailed lazily in the sky. Then there was a clap of thunder, the rain danced down on our immediate neighborhood drenching everything. When the rain fizzled out, no trace of the clouds could be detected in the azur-blue sky. The sun stood in the sky and laughed at the birds chasing the rain drops.

We had a nice crop of hay, and the bales were put into the barn. I was share cropping. The wheat looked simply gorgeous. The farmers who were ploughing, seeding, and harrowing had worked out an itinerary late in the winter (cooperative farming), so that as soon as a field got dry enough for ploughing, it was done. Now the wheat was ripening in that order. But, because of the general drought the fields became ready for harvest almost at the same time. This meant that every man, woman and child, had to pitch in and I was no exception.

I owe my life to Jesus--You also?

The question was: what could I do? I would have to learn how to drive the truck with a flat bed trailer, so it could be loaded with the bales of straw, or ever-so-often with bags of wheat. While the men were unloading the trailer, I would run into the house where we worked and look after my baby. By five o'clock we had reached my fields. Once the sun had set everything began to turn damp. I was asked to make a decision whether to go on and risk having the grain turn hot, or call it off to be finished tomorrow. I told them that the Lord had decreed that it be done today. Every one worked feverishly and without a pause. The straw was baled, and the wheat bagged, someone came with a second combine.

By 10 P.M. I rolled the last load to the barn. The men took their time, carefully separating each bag for air circulation, so that they would not lean on each other. I accompanied them to their tractors... As we came out into the open, we froze ...

We were totally unprepared ... we stared incredulously in the direction of the fields we had just vacated. We were petrified by what we saw:
An enormous steam roller of a white cloud was rolling down the valley and over the fields we had harvested. One of the farmers jumped back down from his tractor, ran to the barn door and closed it as tightly as possible. The others hurridly rumbled out into the night to secure theirs. The last ones out were swallowed by the fog. Huge wisps of fog lunged out at me as I ran into the house. I hugged my patient baby and cried! What, if I had not heeded the Lord? Now all our crops were safely in the barns, and here was the rain we had waited for so long.

None of us, however, realized the full extent of God's blessings, for it began to rain and would not stop. It rained every single day for the next 10 weeks, thundering and lightning at an average temperature of 90 degrees. Wheat still out in the field was flattened to the ground and the kernels began sprouting where they fell. Wheat in shocks ready for threshing, could only be used for silage, for the grains on the stalk began to sprout where they were, and the shocks grew long green hair.

All the farmers made at least two rounds each day digging into the bags of wheat for heat. It became clear already on the second day that most of the wheat cut that day before 9 A.M. and after 5 P.M., that was all of mine, had a raised temperature by the fourth testing. They had already requested time at the mill to run our bags through the dryer. They also turned the last bales of straw and opened some of them, lest they spoil.

Since I had no design on using the wheat, it remained in my barn in excellent shape. In the winter, when the time came to purchase new seeds, none was obtainable. Therefore the farmers decided to purchase mine for our fields, come springtime. In March farmers came from far away paying premium prices for the hay and straw in my barn.

Thanks be to God for his providence!

A country which does not honor the farmer, and does not appreciate the fruits of the field, has not heard God's promise. It is the duty of a nation like ours to make certain that its farmer can make a good living from his labor on the land. He is entitled to a good life without anxiety for the well-being of his family and the future of his land! On the well-being of the farmer hinges the welfare of our Nation ... unions, armies, all are worthless if they lack food.

49: We too belong to His race

ACTS 17, 25-29:
"...for it is HE who gives life and breath and all things
to all men. All Nations HE has created from a common
origin to dwell over the earth ... meaning them to seek
for God on the chance of finding Him ... Though indeed
HE is close to each one of us, for it is in Him that we
live and move and exist ... We too belong to His race."

In the Broad Street subway in the city of brotherly
love, a blue collar worker got up from his seat ready to
step through the door when it opened. The train stopped
and the man took a step forward. That same instant he was
pushed back into the car by a "gentleman" in a black
pin-striped suit with vest, tie and hat. He stuck his
newspaper into the right pocket and began to belabor the
worker with both hands aiming at the ears. The lunch box
tumbled to the floor. He kept shouting epitaphs at his
victim: "You swine, you n@*#, you D#@*&, what makes you
think you have the right to knock me out of the car, you
sk@*#, you useless creature, I'll teach you a lesson.

When the "gentleman" finally let go of his victim, it was
because the doors had closed again, and the train started
in motion ... he had to hold on to something or fall on his
victim. The subway was not empty ... that was the hardest
to bear: No one said a word. No one got up and told that
brute off. The black man sat down dazed and speechless
... he picked up his lunch box.

I collected my thoughts, "this was a free country? Even
in Nazi Germany a person trying to vacate a train had the
right-of-way ... this man was the only one to leave! Now
he had missed his stop and was battered and shaken. Is
that justice?"

Like no other people in the whole world, Americans seem
to thrive on prejudice. Is it that the average, rich and
poor, has no knowledge of the Lord? Is that why they come

to the conviction that the other person or people must be equally prejudiced?

I received a call from the Lord to join the Fellowship Commission, where I was welcomed by Marjorie Penney to help build the Fellowship House. On Sundays we made the rounds to various churches. I sat at the same table with the Reverend Martin Luther King, Jr. when he first started his great mission. We went in a group to plays, movies, restaurants, and sometimes we were booted out and sometimes we could stay. The greatest fun was to convince the department stores that a well trained cosmetician and sales clerk would enhance the sales of cosmetics.

All department stores were short of sales clerks. Wanamakers had advertised, and several of us, including a well-trained black beauty, applied for the job. We, who knew nothing about lip stick and make-up, with no idea what belonged on the counter, received the jobs, while the only qualified person was rejected.

A complaint was filed with the commission ... the hiring practices were exposed. Finally the young woman received the position on trial basis: "If the volume of her counter should drop, Wanamakers were granted to replace her; if the volume remained, she would receive permanent status within three months."

Now the telephones were busy. One person would make six calls on the list and each of those were asked to call six others. We enlisted the aid of the fur-bearing crowd, letting them know about that particular counter at Wanamakers and gave them her hours. The girl was kept busy from opening till closing, and her sales tripled. Already after the first month Wanamakers capitulated. She received permanent status, and they let us recommend a couple of other sales clerks for other departments.

Philadelphia was threatened by a streetcar strike. Because of the economic boom, and the aftermath of the war, there was a decided shortage of conductors and ads remained unanswered. Therefore the company selected three fully qualified black men to be trained.

At the first trial run the white conductors threw the towel into the ring, they turned out en masse, and were ready to stone the black men. One streetcar was already derailed, and they were about to overturn the second, when Marjorie Penney and a press of people, mostly women, descended into the fray, demanding arbitration. That was finally granted. The verbal battle raged for two and one half days.

We were told that citizens would not entrust their lives into the hands of a **black** conductor. Marjorie Penney agreed: "If true, they can be legally fired after the first full week after training."

Three days later everything was set for a trial run. We all boarded the three street cars till no one could drop, paid our fare, and sang the whole way to the Navy Yard and back. Then shifts were organized and the telephones kept busy to let every one know the numbers, and the schedules of the three street cars. People who had not been on the street car in years, took their children for a ride. I think the Transit Authorities had never seen street cars as crowded during off hours as those three street cars during that trial month.

Working as a part of the Fellowship House was lots of fun, and I made a lot of new friends. The triumph was when Marjory Penney won a share of the Nobel Peace Prize, which enabled us to purchase a very fine new building.

However, nothing could substitute for those struggling beginnings in Brown Street, when every individual counted as much as working for the Lord in Berlin.

50: Man is sinful by nature

ISAIAH 43, 24-26:
"No, you have burdened me with sins, and wearied me with your iniquities. Yet it is I who blot out your ill deeds, I put your sins out of my mind; recall to me, in your defense, a single item proving you innocent!"

I had to learn that children are not by nature good and free of evil designs. In nature, I had observed that baby chicks and weasel babies could run circles through the fence and around each mother basking in the sun, without the hen pecking the weasel babies or the weasel mother doing away with a chick. There is a peace and a truth which lets the very young enjoy the benefits of their innocence. Not so human beings, not so my child of barely 18 months.

It had been difficult to acquire a kitten in this rural area, but finally the animal shelter called me: "We have a healthy mother cat, do you want her? In due time we had six kittens, well established outside in the barn. Soon the little ones followed me and my baby everywhere, and he liked to play with them. But then only five showed up, and the sixth could not be found; soon there were only four.
From this day on I watched them very intently, and one day, busy in the barn, I caught my little one catching one of the trusting kittens, and throwing it out of the barn loft. I took him into my arms and went around below. I told him about life, and tried to impress him with the finalty of his miserable deed.

From now on the three kittens followed us to the house, and when I washed in the wash house, or was canning, they were underfoot; when I hung the laundry on the line, they tumbled on the grass. When twelve weeks old or so, all three kittens disappeared on one and the same day. There was no trace of them. I asked my little one. Not a clue...!

=123=

I owe my life to Jesus--You also?

Weeks later the potatoes were ready, plowed out for the picking, and I needed the metal bushel basket, up-side-down near the washing machine. I lifted it up, and there, underneath, lay the three kittens, dried out, starved to death. I looked at my baby at my side ... my heart stood still ... he knew. Lord have mercy on my beloved one!

I tried to bring up my child as best as I knew. I hoped I could bring him onto a righteous path; I watched him closer, but this was very difficult because he was mature for his age, very open and friendly by nature. During the summer we were out on the farm together. As an only child I felt he should have company. Therefore I picked up needy children from the Social Service department of the church in the city. These children stayed from two to eight weeks. This was lots of fun, and he played well with his guests. During the winter he went to an accredited nursery school, run by the city, where he spent between six to eight hours a day while I was on nursing cases or at home. He got on well with the teachers and the children, and loved to entertain them and make them laugh. Then he went to an excellent private school.

After the third grade he went to the public school for the first time ... we had moved to a new community. He was far ahead in all his subjects; his classroom teacher endeavored to teach him orderliness and neatness ...! It smacked of the trivia my mother had wanted me to learn by teaching me etiquette ... nothing to feed a growing mind and soul. Unfortunately we had moved into an established neighborhood with a dozen children his age who had grown up together with an established pecking order. He was not accepted. Having been a single child he was used to taking the lead and the responsibility. But these were not underprivileged children, neither trained to take on responsibility for others, nor for their own conduct. These children were used to getting their every whim, and any means to get their wishes was in order.

Things became even more difficult for the eight year old to handle, because the parents of these children did not accept his mother. They pressed me hard to answer for the crimes committed against the Jews in Nazi Germany, and in the course of events questioned my methods of raising my child. They even came out openly pitying the child for having such a mother.

Without consideration and love for the child, these very same neighbors took it upon themselves to "raise" my child as they saw fit. In doing so, they also solicited their children to monitor mine, so that they could supply that which they thought had to be lacking because of his mother.

In a way, that was the basic technique the Nazis had applied, only, the latter were not quite so overt! You know what had to happen next. Everything and anything was blamed on this child, as long as it was convenient and would avert suspicion from themselves. In the end it did not matter whether mine was present or not.

"Lord, have mercy upon me, and do not mislead me to be unjust, or let my pride be an obstacle. Show me a way to help this child, and lead him on righteous pathways for Thy name's sake." I prayed in tongues that God would help the child to separate right from wrong, and help me to commit no injustice. It is so easy to take sides under pressure, to trust, or to condemn the child. With the help of the Lord I withheld judgement in issues I did not witness, in others I trusted my child rather than the neighbors, especially as long as no adult had actually witnessed it.

Of course, my child, like yours, was by no means without reproof, and the Lord had ways to lead me to evidence, sometimes immediately. For instance, to make friends, he rifled our coin collection and bartered them with a neighbor; the Lord led me to turn over flower pots which served as way stations ... the rest was easy. When he had cheated me I found proof sometimes within the hour.

As a normal boy, unfortunately, he tried to get even with his peers for being slighted, which made matters worse. Later on he turned to others outside the community, where it was impossible to keep an eye on him. He stole things from the girls and secreted them away outside. Then I experienced what you women suffer, when you are standing alone trying to raise up sons. A growing lad needs an understanding father who encourages him and upholds him, and still is firm and just. His father was sick, especially on weekends and holidays. He needed drugs to function. As an American he was well liked in the community, but he himself had no need for friends. Ever since the birth of the child the man felt slighted, and jealous of him, rather than taking a stake in his nurture. Perhaps in trying to avoid committing the same mistake my mother had committed in keeping my father away from us children, I leaned backwards to find opportunities to have these two become acquainted. NO ONE can teach another to love. You must want to! Christ can only help those who sincerely seek him. Love is a two-way bond!

Each generation tries to avoid or correct the mistakes committed by the one before, and thus creates their own. The players are of different nature. While my father was very mature and very responsible, my husband was neither. He had married to be taken care of, he despised himself and was filled with guilt! I forced on him responsibilities he never wanted.

"Lord, forgive my guilt ... I had wanted so badly to do the right things, and to be worthy of your trust. Without YOUR guidance, I know, it would have been an outright disaster ... I would, however, feel better, if I could have the confidence, that YOU, my Lord, are his Lord also ... I am just a mother, Lord! Forgive me: **Thy will be done on earth ..."**

51: I shall lead you to a new land

PSALM 105, 42-45; PSALM 106, 1:
"So he brought his people out with joy ... Halleluja!
Give thanks to the Eternal! ... he is good, his kindness
never fails..."

My father had survived the conflagration, experiments
with X-Ray therapy, neglect, and X-Ray burns. The cancer
was dead, but half of his hip-bone also. He had survived
42 major operations, not counting the removal of many bone
splinters. Finally plastic surgery succeeded. By end of 1947
he was given permission to travel to join us here in the
United States.

On January 5, 1948, we were called to New York to
welcome the first immigration boat from Europe to touch our
shores. My parents were on board.
I was among the few asked to represent Church World
Relief. We climbed on board of the pilot boat and rode out
to meet the huge British Queens ship with the customs and
immigration officials.
Our impressions are hard to describe: Among the
thousand passengers there was hardly a person between the
ages of 14 and 55; only children or grandparents. All had
relatives in the U.S. All had suffered under the Nazis and
the holocaust of war. The children were in deplorable
condition. About a third of the people carried on their
backs their total possessions. We had the authority to check
any suitcase to assess their need, estimate the size of the
person, and pin various tags on his coat for identification
eliminating duplicate questions. Take, for instance, a frail
grandmother with three little ones, carrying a large
suitcase with apparent ease. I had her open it. It contained
a worn Bible, a dictionary, a pair of gloves without
fingers, a shop-worn doll of doubtful color ... no wonder
she could carry it. Other grandparents came with one, or
two little ones in a baby buggy, including their earthly
possessions. Many children had to be channeled to a
hospital center to be quarantined for fear they might not
survive an exposure to measles.

I owe my life to Jesus--You also?

Everything was well organized to receive these folks. Every need was anticipated by the churches of New York. There were pick-up centers, centers for unaccompanied younsters, those with babies, overnight facilities, food and clothing sorted by sizes down to layettes and diapers. There was an overlap, but channeling was important. Need was the deciding factor for the right bus to the right church. On the ship I was strictly one of the workers. My parents, of course, were on my list: after almost ten years ... I pinned tags on them to ride with me and my charges ... I had to tear myself away ... on to the next.

Suddenly a hush fell over the crowd. The huge liner tilted noticably. Every one, even the littlest sank down on their knees. The band played our national anthem ... hands stretched up to the Lord in thanksgiving. We passed the Statue of Liberty.

By the time the ship was pushed into the pier, the immigration officials had done their job. The people waited at ten or more exits on the several levels as they appeared on the list, and indicated by the color of their tags. When the gang planks went down, discharge was very fast. Each group was received by a worker leading them to waiting cars and busses. Now I had mother and father at my side. What an overwhelming feeling! My husband and their only grandchild were waiting at the center.

Other heart-breaking scenes all around us ... here all the loved ones were waiting. What a welcoming! Interpreters were needed ... one grandmother repeated over and over: "You want to say we can pick any piece of clothing we like?" ... "Yes, but try it on first, make sure it fits!" Trash cans were filled with rags.

The farm had been winterized, and turned over to my folks. When June came they loved to sit in the sun on the lawn near the tall lilies, just as seen in the dream on the Mountain of Our Lady many years ago.

"For he remembered his own sacred pledge ...
Halleluja! Give thanks to the Eternal!
He is good, His kindness never fails."

52: Pray for us too, brothers in Christ

ROMANS 16, 1-16; and 16,4:
"Let me introduce our sister Phoebe, a deaconess ...
receive one another ... She has been a help herself to
many people..." -- "Salute my fellow-workers in Christ
Jesus, who have risked their lives ... Thank them and
all the Gentile churches as well ... the congregation that
meets in their house."

"I", said the Lord one day in 1949, "I will send you to
your brothers and sisters behind the Iron Curtain and to
my people in the Middle East, that you may comfort them
and tell them to be steadfast in their belief. Tell them
greetings from my people in the United States that they are
remembered in their prayers."

"Lord," I answered, "you waste your breath on the
wrong person ... as it stands, I have afforded myself but
the bare essentials. I have hardly enough to clothe myself
and the child, I have trouble finding enough funds to
support my parents, and thirdly, I know nothing about the
countries and their peoples. You know, my health is rotten
... You let thirty hornets sting me and poison my system;
You let me have a vicious attack of poison ivy, that I
cannot sleep, nor wake, with eyes swollen shut. This is
now the third month. If You are serious, lots of thing must
be changed first!"

You heard the Lord's command, and my honest answer.
It had seemed no end to the sting and poison ivy plague,
but now, one week was enough to clear it up. Then my
brother received his visa and joined my parents. We moved,
leaving the farm to my folks.

The Lord led me to Dr. Vanderbilt; she asked me:
"Since when do you have the trouble with sleeping?"
"Since I was stung by thirty-two hornets!"
"Let me look at you! This is a miracle of the Lord that
you are still alive! ... Your metabolism is upset ... let me
take your blood pressure ... 68 over 90, I cannot see how

you can function! ... Here is a prescription, this might be all you need. Meanwhile, I'll set up an appointment for a metabolism test at the hospital."

That took care of my physical problems. Next I discovered that Benjamin Franklin's library had a strong Middle East section, so I "dug in".

Meanwhile, I received a well-paying position as a blouse designer. To go to work I needed a car. At the time Grandpa Eckert was sick and could no longer drive his car, while his doctor bills mounted up. I made a visit to his farm and checked the car, a sparkling black, antique Dodge, in almost new condition. The engine had been overhauled at 55,000 miles. It had years of love and care inside a garage. The market value was low, I needed a dependable car ... this was it. They needed financial help. I offered him one fourth more than the market value, and he relinguished the keys dismissing me with God's blessings. He was right, it was a good car lasting me another 75,000 miles without a repair job.

A year later my father was informed that he was reinstated and was again receiving his due retirement checks payable to an escrow account in Germany, his to claim anytime upon return. At the same time the City of Essen bought the ground of a bombed out estate, of which my mother received one sixth. That, too, was paid into an escrow account.

Meanwhile, my father developed bladder trouble which could not be identified. They talked about cancer between the bladder and the kidney. As we all know, medical costs are prohibitive in this country. Therefore, he decided to cross the ocean and prepare a place for my mother to follow him. After five years in this country my mother followed him.

That fall my husband came home with the news that he was receiving a sabbatical year, and that he had signed up for an orientation trip to the Middle East. I said: "That is fine, the child and I are going along."

"From where are the finances for you and the boy to come?" he asked.

"I have the necessary money in my account."

Indeed, I was well prepared for the trip, I knew the land as it had been in ancient times, at the time of Christ, and what I could expect at present. Searching, as I did, however, I had been totally unsuccessful in finding out anything about present-day Christian communities. Now I requested letters of introduction from the various denominations to their congregations in the Middle East, in Yugoslavia, in Turkey and in Egypt.

We decided that we would follow the trip of St. Paul, just backwards, starting in Rome. For this rugged trip we bought a Willys station wagon. We obtained all the shots, and visas. In early Spring 1955 we went on our way.

The trip was very hard on my husband. He was frequently out of commission with migrane headaches and drug-related symptoms. Often, when we arrived at sister congregations, he was not able to function. I knew my command from the Lord. I was prepared, and I was never refused. In Yugoslavia I spoke to an audience of over 600 people, mostly woman. They came from all over on less than three hours' notice, and we had a different crowd at church again on the following morning at 6 A.M. before work. We were welcomed thus in Turkey, in Lebanon, Syrian, Jordan and Egypt.

I have learned a lot about Christian communities in the Middle East. They are a minority of 10% in all the Arab countries except for Lebanon and Egypt where the percentage is higher. There are very few converts; most of them held steadfast to the faith of their fathers since Christ had walked the earth. Their fathers have survived many trials and ordeals for their faith in Jesus Christ, and they are willing to follow in their footsteps. They were proud people, conscious of their faith. During the ages their ancestors had fled to the caves when pressured too much. They felt, they too, could do the same and eke out a living until it was safe to return again into the village. For centuries they had to pay a head-tax from which a Moslem was exempted. At other times they have lived and worked in good relationship with non-Christians under one village government made up of the Christian priest and the Mohammedan leader.

Our Palestinian brethren in Christ were living in great distress. Their personal property, as well as the property of the Christian Churches had been at least 80% confiscated. This was a process still going on while I was with them. Bombs were planted in one housing complex. The families fled with little but their children during the wee hours of the night; without clothing -- as they were. When they returned, the embers still hot, they found the fires out with limited damage. But their houses were boarded up and signs posted informing the owners that the houses were confiscated as abandoned. I investigated such an incident in company of the United Nations forces.

Over and over they asked me the question: "Why are the American people trying to punish us? Our fathers have lived in this village for at least two thousand years. As long as memory reaches, the land has belonged to the same families. A village does not turn Christian over night. We have always been Christian. Will you let the Americans know?"

ACTS 7, 47:
"(God gave) permission to devise a dwelling for the God of Jacob. It was Solomon who built him a house. And yet the most High does not dwell in houses made by hands; as the prophet says: 'Heaven is my throne, the earth is a footstool for my feet! On what spot could I settle? Did not my hand make all this? Stiff-necked, uncircumcised in heart and ear, you are always resisting the holy Spirit.'"

"Tell your Churches in America: You have taken our property, our communities broken up and scattered. Why do

you persecute us? Even now you surge upon us with arms
made in the U.S.A. threatening to wipe us from the earth.
We have not been compensated for our land, our houses or
their contents. We have not hurt a soul. We have been
peacefully minding our business as our fathers before us."

I was stunned ... I had no reply. Where should the
people go? Palestine is about 270 miles long and at the most
just 60 miles wide. Desert is hemming the Palestinian coast.
There are 32 miles at the most between the desert and the
Mediterranean. The hills of Judah are barren and
undesirable for human settlements. The coast lands of the
Philistians were cleared at gun point. I have heard no
zealous American ever asking about their Christian
brethren, or caring about their livelihood. Believe me, I
have seen the misery with my own eyes. God is not with
guns and war machinery ... it may be slow in coming, but
a day of reckoning is inevitable. There is still time to
repent and mend our way ... when it is upon us, it will be
too late. Thus says the Lord through the Prophet Micah:

**MICAH 4, 3-4: "He will decide disputes of many races, and
arbitrate between strong foreign powers, till swords are
beaten into ploughshares, spears into pruning-hooks; no
nation points the guns against another, no longer shall men
learn to fight ... but live ... in terror of no one..."**

But the body of Christ is one body:
1 CORINTHIANS 12, 26:
   **"Thus if one member suffers, all the members share its
   suffering; if one member is honored, all members share
   its honor. Now you are Christ's Body, and severally
   members of it."**
Then the Lord added:
2 CORINTHIANS 13, 11:
   **"Now, brothers, good-bye; mend your ways, listen to
   what I have told you, live in harmony, keep the peace;
   then the God of love and peace will be with you."**

"Dear Lord", I answered to the Lord, "if this is the
message I am to broadcast to the congregations in the
United States, they will cast me out ... I with my defective

speech and tainted ancestry! I shall never receive a
hearing, the presses are biased against those, thy people!
Do I have not trouble enough?"

The Lord does not enter arguments! All I have to say is
that I sympathize with Jonah. I did not fight it, I spoke to
a good number of churches, to associations, and in schools,
in Germany and in this country. No one wants this kind of
news. To the contrary, our churches are excited about
rebuilding the Lord's temple, and establishing **HIS KINGDOM
on earth** ... I am ordered to say to you:
> **Your undertaking is foolish ... you cannot confine God
> in a temple, no matter how splendid! ... Neither can
> you confine God's people in a plot of land of the size of
> Washington, D.C. and immediate suburbs. Those who
> believe in ME and in MY SON, YOUR LORD JESUS
> CHRIST, ARE MY PEOPLE!"**

This stands to reason: discounting the desert, sixty-six
square miles is a tiny plot of land, even if paved with
gold, silver and jewelry. Think of it, a man can cross this
territory in ten hours on foot, by bicycle in two hours, a
car can cross it in half an hour, a plane in seconds. There
is not enough room for the indigenous population to make a
living. Instead of paving it with blessings, we surround it
with guns as if to keep love out. We are sacrificing our
national resources to seed strife. The Lord does not need
war machinery to defend himself ... man devises his own
ruin.

53: Lord, why do you pick on me?

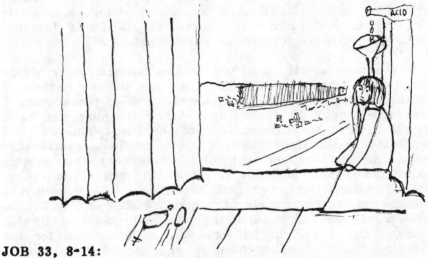

JOB 33, 8-14:
"You argued, in my hearing, for I heard you claim ... I
am pure and sinless ... but God picks a quarrel with
me, he treats me as his enemy, he fastens logs to my
feet, he watches every step I take; and if I cry, he will
not answer:..."

The Lord let me be bitten by a spider, he sent me bed
bugs, and he let me be eaten up by a swarm of mosquitoes.
By the time I had reached the pinnacles of the Acropolis in
Athens I felt as if I were dragged through hell. It felt as
if someone had pushed a funnel into my head and was
dribbling acid into my veins. I had the chills sitting in the
hot sun. I knew that was more than I could handle in a
tent.

My husband drove me to the sparkling new American
hospital. Someone popped a thermometer into my mouth and
promptly forgot about me. The chills had left me, and the
heat had not yet started. A doctor came and took a reading
... it was normal. He explained that this hospital could not

keep me, even if I were very sick, "the hospital is to accommodated only the armed forces and their dependents." He looked at my mottled skin and added: "Here is a bottle of Calomine, just in case it should itch ... if this does not help, you will have to turn to a Greek doctor."

I dragged myself back out of the hospital. Our abode was a tent on the site of Pireaus, the ancient harbor of Athens, near the beach. In the wee hours of the morning I awakened enough to realize that not everything was as it should be with the hand-maiden of the Lord. The acid had permeated to the finger tips; I could hardly move ... stiff from head to toe, and painful. I found the thermometer taken along for the child. I labored to get it under my arm. The flashlight revealed the time, 4 A.M. When I remembered the thermometer the hand pointed to 5 A.M. ... the reading said 105, and the sun had not done it! My husband and the child felt cold ... probably not too far from the truth. I woke them up and kidded them that it would take me three hours to dress myself. Fear chased them into the dawn to find a Greek doctor.

I barely managed to put on the most necessary, when they were already back with the news that they had a doctor waiting at a certain corner in Athens for a ride to his office. It was 7 A.M. Somehow they got me on the back seat of the car; the street corner was found, and I was transferred to a couch in the office.

"Your first day?"

"Since yesterday about noon," I told him about the bottle of Calomine. He smiled: "Well, they are not familiar with the diseases common around here. I want you to sign this paper, permission to treat you and to place you into a hospital, which in Athens, is very difficult because every bed is filled."

"What do you think I have?"

"I am very glad you put it that way, because, if I treat you my way, we will never know for certain. But if you had been taken to the new American Base Hospital, they

=136=

would have waited for proof from the laboratory. That takes
a good five days for a culture in the test tube. By then it
is too late for help of any kind. What I think you most
certainly have is spinal meningitis. The tell‑tale symptoms:
the high fever ... the pain ... and the stiffness; all are
there."

"I'll sign! ... No thank you! I don't need proof! Start
the treatment!"

The nurse handed him a syringe and two bottles, one
with penicillin, the other with terramycin: both had
superimposed in bold letters: **World Church Relief; do not
use after August 1953** ... it did not matter to me, but I
thought this was 1955 already

THANKS FOR THE MEDICINE, WORLD CHURCH RELIEF!

The doctor gave me the maximum doses recommended
from each. Then he looked for sulfa tablets. We had them
in the car, just for an emergency ... the doctor was
pleased. Meanwhile, his secretary spent hours on the phone
before locating an empty bed. The doctor was not too
happy about the particular hospital: "Don't be shocked, it
does not come close to meeting American standards, it is
not really sanitary, the food is deplorable, I will specify
that your food be brought from a restaurant. However, you
will have good care," he added wistfully, "probably no one
speaks English!"

Nobody did; but by that time I was stretched out in the
bed and for the next three days I had absolutely no wishes
... lemonade without sugar. Slowly the pain receded, I
could think of moving again, and of food. The doctor
stopped in for all the medication personally, that dear soul!
Then he ordered rice with chicken, explaining it in Greek.
Heads nodded. Faces beamed. They promised to find the
chicken. That was at 6 P.M.; at 7 P.M. some one brought
the rice. It turned cold. They had sent out to the
restaurants, but they were still closed. (The Greeks don't
think of eating until 10 or 11 at night.) By 8 P.M. they
had hit upon a compromise, they brought the "chicken" still
... in the shell ... an egg to go with my rice. Despite my

troubles my laughter brought tears to my eyes.

The doctor had done it! One week later he could dismiss me. He even had made arrangements for me in the brand new Y.W.C.A. with an American style cafeteria, supervised by high society women. They went out of their way to make me welcome. They wanted to know the name of my doctor. "Oh yes, he is excellent! He is the personal physician of the Queen."

One week later the doctor discharged me happily. "Praise the Lord, you were very fortunate that they did not keep you at the new American Hospital. On the day you came into my hands they also had a woman come to them in identical condition. When you left the hospital they had not yet begun to treat her, still waiting for the laboratory results; I am on their advisory staff. Now she has no longer a chance. It is much too late, she is in a coma."

"Which of these three drugs, do you think, did the trick?"
He laughed, "truly, I have never given it a thought, but the three together have done it each time, and then, of course, prayers!"

We hugged each other, and my husband and my child welcomed me back. It seems that the Lord had wanted me to get an insight into the problems which beset Greece, that could not be done any other way.
THE LORD'S WAYS ARE MARVELOUS AND STRANGE!

God had another design. HE delayed our entrance into Istanbul just long enough to have us miss the terrible purge of Greeks. When we arrived it was just in time to wipe the tears of our Christian brethren and sisters, hurt or unharmed. They will be steadfast in the Lord, as their forefathers had pledged to St. Paul.

54: What rises is immortal

1 CORINTHIANS 13, 1-8:
**"Thus I may speak with the tongues of men and of
angels, but have no love I am a noisy gong or a
clanging cymbal; ...Love is very patient, very kind.
Love knows no jealousy; ...Love never disappears."**

The Lord had given me a dear, dear friend. Mary lived
just three houses away ... she was the sunshine of the
community. The two of us became friends the day we met.
Mary was very industrious and could make something others
considered trash into something worthwhile and pretty; and
so could I. We talked about LAST THINGS. She had been
brought up a Catholic, but for Chet's sake they both had
joined the Friends Meeting. Therefore she said to me: "Yes,
Hildegard, I believe that Christ is with us and that there is
life after death. I am worried about Chet, he wants to hear
nothing of it. I know I will meet up with my Redeemer. But
let's talk about something else, such thoughts make Chet
unhappy."

When I returned from our trip two years later, Mary and
I were happy and relieved to be together again. We needed
each other in every respect. She was not well, and I was
prone to all common viruses and resistant to all types of
drugs. We hardly had to use the telephone, we knew when
we were needed. Mary was a registered nurse and hovered
over me in a crisis like an angel. At other times I was with
Mary.

You see, Mary had also worked as an X-Ray technician
both before she was married and also afterwards. Then
X-Rays were in their infancy, and nobody thought much
about the fact that the laboratory was underneath the
X-Ray machine. When she became pregnant, the fetus
became sterilized in her womb, and fossilized, until it was
expelled by accident two years later. Now, twenty years
later, nothing was functioning properly.

In January, when I stopped in as usual, Mary could not
get out of her seat. I sat on the floor and held her hand,

words flowed without moving the lips. Then I got up and said: "Does the doctor know that you are in terrible pain? I'll talk with her, you need relief." She nodded and I drove into the night. The last patient had just left, and we discussed the problem. The doctor agreed, Mary should not suffer. By the time I returned the prescription was delivered.

Mary went to the hospital for blood transfusions. One time she returned with the chills. We never really talked in words about anything like that, you would have seen us smile, shrug the shoulders, shake heads and nod. "The wrong blood type, so what? The next time you need one it would speed you on the way to the Lord." She gave in to the doctors to make an exploratory operation. We could communicate with each other, distance did not really matter. She called me every morning just to hear my voice, or vice versa. They had shortened the bone of the hip, and put her into a cast from the arm pit to the knee ... a hellish torture, which was given up four weeks later as futile. She wanted to be home for her birthday and Easter. I had a telephone installed next to the hospital bed in the living room within 24 hours ... thanks to the Bell Telephone Company ... Mary loved it.

Meanwhile I had gone back to designing blouses. The head cutter, the most important person for a designer, and I worked together to a degree which was unreal. If he was in conference and needed a pattern, I would walk in with that particular one. If I was stuck for any reason, he would produce the missing link without losing time. As children of God we knew how to communicate without words. I knew his family, and he mine. What we could have accomplished, had we met before marriage!

Mary, however, lasted hardly a week at home. She consented to another operation ... I called her and asked her: "Mary, do you want me to come over to see you off?"
"No, Hildegard, we'd go to pieces, you know too much ... I am not scared. If I have a wish, I'll let you know in time."

=140=

I owe my life to Jesus--You also?

The operation took place at 8:30 A.M. the next morning. I was at work, and knew that things went exactly the way Mary and I knew they would go ...: badly. She was moved into the recovery room. I was at home when I received Mary's request: "Hildegard, prepare my mother and Chet!" ... That was superhuman.

I talked with the recovery room nurse, she was getting a blood transfusion. Every one was optimistic about the outcome. At 10 P.M. I called her mother for a long talk. She had come from the hospital. "No, everything was fine, and Chet was sent home for the night."
Minutes later what I had said hit home ... My telephone rang ... a desperate mother: "I want my girl, my only girl!" ... "In Christ's name!"

At last I reached Chet. He scolded me for taking his peace. "Mary was resting, and the doctors found everything according to expectation. It is late." He hung up ... that was understandable.
At six o'clock Chet called me back; this time from the hospital. "They had wanted me at Mary's side at 4 A.M. I'll call you before you leave for work. He did ... Mary was in a coma.
About an hour later, I had just arrived at work ready for my first design, when I looked at the head cutter. He said: "I can feel it, something has happened."
"You know, right now Mary has died."
He went about his business, but in passing he said:"Go and call the hospital."
I did. It was 17 minutes to 9 A.M.; the chief nurse from the recovery room answered, I recognized her voice and she mine: "Mary has died, has she?"
"No, I have come off the floor this very minute; she was talking to Chet..." She paused: "Hold on! I will go in and check for you!" The time clock at my elbow ticked away the interminable length of two minutes before her voice returned: "Yes, Mary died five minutes ago."

55: Ask, seek, knock; trust you'll succeed!

ACTS 9, 11-12, 15:
"... And the Lord said to him: "Go to the street called 'Straight street' ... He is praying at this very moment, and he has seen a man called Ananias enter and lay his hands upon him to bring back his sight ... Go; I have chosen him..."

I have walked and talked with the Lord all my life; I have rejoiced when a soul had found him, and I knew I was not meant to keep Him to myself. Christ meant for me to let all of you know about His wisdom, and His anxiousness to help you too! I had to find the Lord's people, and I needed the Lord to tell me where to look, like Ananias to find Paul. A new congregation was founded not far from home. The established parishes looked at it askance, too charismatic. That is where the Lord led my feet.

Ernie Schmidt was my Ananias, he knew the power of prayer; he had learned it from his grandmother. She had an older son who was serving in World War II ... somewhere in Europe. His grandmother was preparing a meal. Suddenly she was clutching her heart and cried out: "Lord, please help my son! I want my son back!" and then weeping. A long time later they received word that he was lost in the war. Ernie Schmidt's church became my first church home in this country.

What makes a Church a HOME? It is the common concern, the common goals which bind a family, not just on Sundays, but day in and day out, whether all the members are at home, at work, or out for fun. It is the same whether a family consists of three members, or twenty members, or 1500 members. Jesus Christ is our brother, and our Lord God is the FATHER. Ernie Schmidt, one of our brothers, preached sermons not at a congregation, but to the individual member of the family, teaching that Christ is walking with each one of us. He reinforced my faith, that the Lord is listening to each of us, answering our requests. You must expect an answer! When you talk on the telephone, don't you expect an answer?

The Lord is as powerful as we make Him. If you are fearful, timid, afraid to disturb Him, even if you trust Him only a little bit, you will get just a little bit. If you are bold and courageous, and put all your trust and faith in Him, you get much, and you may claim more and more.

Since we are all children of one God, and He is our Father, it is proper to look at an ideal father on earth for comparison. His children are His obligation, His charges, we are His dependents. The only difference is that God's resources are not only unlimited; He also knows where they are, and how to put them to best advantage for the benefit of all the family, not just for the individual himself. HE knows the most advantageous time.

Let us consider an ideal parent-child relationship: ninety-nine times out of a hundred the child has minor requests from a parent, for example:
"Will you be home when school is out? I have a splinter in my finger ... my shoes are getting too tight ... Do you want to listen to something funny? I have to be at the dentist's. I need help with the tuition. I have to have something to wear at the prom."
None of these questions are well formulated; neither are

=143=

the answers. Occasionally you meet a wise parent who sits down with his child and explains to him the reasons for his decision. However, the decision itself does not ruffle the relationship between parents and children. The more the children come to the parents the happier they are, because this is the sign that their children love them and trust them; they would come to them long before they would seek counsel outside of the family. How much the child receives on freedom, money, status, depends on how much faith the parents have in their child ... Children love the parents, because the parents loved them first.

Now my beloved, GOD is OUR FATHER, HE loved us first, HE has faith in you and me. If you go to the Father and ask him to aid "all the poor and sick", he will shrug his shoulders, and forget about it. It's the same, as if your child would come home from school asking you to sit down with all the children failing and help them with their home work. Children are not that unrealistic to earthly parents. Why be unreasonable in your requests to the Lord? If my shoe pinches, your toes don't hurt!

But if you have promised to pick some one up and you cannot find the car keys, why not ask the Lord: "Please, let me find my keys". The Lord, then, will have a chance to tell you: "Why not look in the ignition!" ... "Oh, thank you Lord", that is were they were, for the Lord knew how much it meant for you to be on time.

When you come to the Lord, our Father, you don't have to explain yourself. Like our earthly parents, He anticipates most of our wishes long before you have put them into words. Formulating wishes is part of the learning process, part of being a child. How often must parents help children to formulate a wish? Do parents answer all the wishes of their children right away? Why expect it from your Father in Heaven?

Let us see how this works: Some years back I had a return flight from Amsterdam in time to teach in college. I had thanked the Lord for this early return ticket. The details were sent to me; everything would be fine. The letter was still sealed, the Lord had not moved me to open it and check the date. When I finally opened the letter it was 10 A.M. on Saturday. Because of my request the agency had pushed my flight two days ahead ... my plane was to depart from Amsterdam at 1:30 P.M. this very afternoon. @#* what to do, I was miles away in Belgium. I called the agency: "No problem, we have plenty of stand-bys. You'll be stand-by #5 for the plane leaving midnight Sunday".

"Thank you Lord, You got me into a pickle!" HE does not answer such things. I think in this case HE must have laughed at me! Anyway, I had a wonderful time that Saturday, and a lovely drive through Holland in bloom.

I was in time for my plane. Stand-by #4 was called, then the gate was closed, and the plane rolled into the night without me. I was happy, I made myself a bed in the wardrobe, and washed myself in the deserted washroom. I was hardly asleep when the loudspeakers began to blare: "Stand by busses, stand by! Take passengers to assigned hotels. Plane maintenance crews: oxygen supply failure ... report immediately to ... Busses stand by, busses ... plane departure 0,24, returning ... maintenance crew report to ..."

Well, I was not on the plane. I turned over and nothing woke me up until the clean-up crew was vaccuuming around my makeshift bed.

All dressed and sparkling I returned to the main hall, where students kept watch over an incredibly high pile of baggage. The airport was swarming with police and soldiers. I kidded one of them: "Are you always guarding your airport like this?"

"Have you not heard the news?"

"What news?"

"On Saturday the plane leaving for New York at 12 noon, and the plane leaving at 1:30 P.M. were both highjacked to Jordan. Now we are two planes short, and the plane put into service at midnight had been pressed into service before being completely checked out."

Brothers, I love the Lord's **NO** as much as His **YES**.

Walking and talking with Christ can be quite rough.

=145=

When Jesus called St. Paul, don't imagine that his troubles were over. Indeed, the opposite was true: before his encounter with Christ, Paul was considered a powerful, up‑ and‑coming young man. And yet, in three days Paul learned to pray to His Father in Heaven; he had met Christ in his full Glory, he was beholding a vision revealing to him the immediate future in every detail. He knew he had a mission, and that communication was possible at all times.

What worked for Paul works for us now!

You will ask: "How is it possible to communicate with the Lord on a daily, yes, on an hourly basis?"

But the answer is quite simple. No age is better equipped than ours to understand communications. Let us assume that our soul was furnished with a T.V. transmitter and a T.V. receiver, and that the main relay station is with God in Heaven. In addition, imagine that the Lord has the most perfect computer system to which all the stations have access on equal time. We, then, are equipped to receive and to send. Yet nothing works, for we have forgotten the power‑hook‑up. The power is the HOLY SPIRIT. We don't have to pay for it, but we still have to turn it on, free for the asking. One cannot see its power, but one learns about it by experimenting. For St. Paul, and Ananias the T.V. transmitter and receivers operated without fault ... to the embarrassment of both men, to Paul as well as Ananias.

What I want to impress upon you is that prayer is communication, and if you put **nonsense** into the computer, it is thrown out as undeliverable. It must be personal, you must want it, and it must be meaningful to you. Then it is readily accepted and stored. It is checked against every possibility and fit into the wishes for you at the heart of your Heavenly Father. When the answer comes back to you it is with your best interest at heart. Sometimes the answer comes back to you even before you are ready for it; sometimes it is thrown out instantly as impractical; and at other times it has a long run before sanctioning, or coming to nought. That is not your worry.

I owe my life to Jesus--You also?

Since we have this in-put and out-put power for communicating with the Lord, and because we operate on the same wave length as God and the angels, we can also train ourselves to tune in on the same wave length as those we love, as well as those we do not know, on earth and in heaven. We can solicit aid of those who have gone before us to help us solve problems in research. But please remember, you cannot communicate with the evil ones, with those who never had the Spirit, or the power of communicating with God in prayer. They are dead.

The devil has to come to the person directly, and you can ask Christ to keep him from you. This wave length is completely safeguarded by the **HOLY SPIRIT**. Praise the Lord! Don't doubt what comes from God, lest you become guilty of refusing to do his will. Ananias had good reason for wishing to stay out of an encounter with a Nazi, persecuting the Church; neither did we in Berlin wish to deal with thirty-five Nazis. If that was what the Lord wished us to do? When a Nazi was separated and sat alone at a table with 11 willing Christians, he, too, had a name, a face, and a soul. God did not ignore his needs, and we knew, that his prayers had joined ours: "Lord, here is Hans, our brother, you have him for two hours, enter his heart." We rejoiced at every sign that God had heard our request. It was a thrill to have HIM with us.

This, my friends, takes me back to my CHURCH HOME with Ernie Schmidt. In his sermons he talked to certain people on subjects we all needed, and then we prayed for those certain people, just as we prayed over every one at our table in Berlin. Yes, we could feel the power which streamed out to the Lord and, truly, you could feel that power flowing back from Jesus Christ. It touched our lives, and created a very happy feeling among this family of God. We have it in us to sustain each other, because the Lord hears and understands us.

Thank you Lord, for those Ernie Schmidts!

56: Let the dead bury the dead
MATTHEW 15, 7-8:

> **You hypocrites, it was indeed of you that Isaiah prophesied when he said: "Since this people draw near me with their mouth," says the Eternal, "honoring me with their lips, while their hearts are far remote; since their religion is a mockery, a mere tradition learned by rote; I will now deal with them to their amazement, bewildering, surprising them, till their wise men lose their wits, and their clever men are fooled."**

The theologian God had entrusted into my care had increasing troubles, nightmares, vision problems, withdrawal symptoms; he had no one to confide in. He despised his father with such a fervor that his name was never mentioned voluntarily. He loved and honored his mother, and for her sake never raised the issue. His father loved to celebrate Christmas, Easter, and birthdays of all the family, including all the friends. Everything which his father loved, the son detested. Therefore, he also detested what was German. When his father died he went dutifully to his mother's side. On his return, he took a clean breath, and said: "I hope when I am that old, I am not such an egotistical and selfish a character." He did it without using the word "father", or his name, and that ended any future reference.

When he lay in embraces, I asked a few times what he was thinking, each time he stiffened and flung himself to the other side of the bed with the words: "That is not your business."
"Why then do you like to cuddle up with me?"
"Stay out of my affairs, mind your own, it is my right, I have given the wedding vow to take care of you."

Sometimes he helped out and delivered an outstanding and beautiful sermon. Afterwards I would ask him: "Those thoughts must fill your heart with peace and gladness, don't they?"
He answered sullenly: "Well, that is all a matter of knowing what the people want to hear."

I owe my life to Jesus--You also?

As the years passed I did no more questioning. Then one Sunday he again had preached a beautiful sermon which meant so much to me that I was deep in thoughts. I passed by in the line-up at the door, shaking hands with the pastor as usual and walking slowly down the steps, when his voice drifted into my thoughts. Looking up into his amused face, I heard him say to his surrounding: "Hey you, I am your husband." I woke up to reality and went back up the stairs, and joined him greeting the people. This happened a second and a third time ... I am not prone to forgetting people. Jesus Christ was left out, his name was seldom used. I remembered my confirmation ... it is not what the preacher does, but the touch of Jesus Christ.

Shortly after Mary had passed on to the Lord, I had a dream. In this vision the Lord showed me to myself in cap and gown graduating from College twice, the second time receiving a degree. HE showed me traveling through France, and celebrating my parents' golden wedding anniversary. He took me through a territory in the United States I had not seen before. I saw myself standing in a classroom before college students teaching, and loving it. Then I asked:

"And what about my husband?"

HE answered me sternly, almost frightningly: "You are to follow me! I have called you by your name ... Let nothing interfere, or deter you ... **Let the dead bury their own dead.**"

Soon thereafter many things I thought impossible were shaping up. My little lad went to a private high school which he detested, but without which he would have rotted. Again his father was sick; he had only one supercilious question: "And who is going to pay for it?"

"I am", was the simple answer.

Thereupon the man relaxed, took a deep breath and a sigh of relief. He replied: "Well, that is fine with me, you will find out he won't amount to much."

That summer I made arrangements to spend three months in France to remove my deficiencies in French, and the

=149=

following summer to do some research.

Back at home I was taking 18 credit hours, I was engaged as substitute teacher, I gave lectures, and later taught French, introducing it in Elementary School. There was little left from my salary to cover the ordinary household expenses. However, when I was absolving my student teaching, I had to give up all income producing activities; then I was hard pressed for funds, and time.

But throughout this very difficult period the Lord kept talking to me. There was no doubt or fear in my soul. HE was preparing me for things to come. The Lord loosened the tight bond between me and my child, preparing us both for an independent role, as painful as it was to both of us to be separated. He gave the child a chance to act and think independently, to realize his own potentials. No other than Christ could have accomplished that. The poor child went nearly berserk over it. Despite his IQ of over 150 he went on a strike, playing the dolt, for which his father held him, and my brother held his hand. He drove to the school persuading him to realize that he did not have the stuff for a college career, that it was foolish to let himself be pushed into this by his mother.
Strange as it may seem, the lad decided not to quit. Instead, he did finish, doing a credible job. Praise the Lord! HE had helped him find his way.

By the time I went to graduate school, the Express Way was built, and the skyline of Philadelphia had changed. One bright and sunny day in March, after I had lost my husband, I sat on that particular stretch I had seen in the dream when my little one was one year old. Suddenly there was metal grinding upon metal behind me. My car was crippled and I sat alone. Finally near midnight it was my son who retrieved me from the scene of the accident.

57: Love is patient and enduring

1 CORINTHIANS 13, 8-10:
"Love never disappears ...For we only know bit by bit,
and we only prophesy bit by bit: but when the perfect
comes, the imperfect will be superseded... at present I
am learning bit by bit, but then I shall understand, as
all along I have myself been understood."

My brother had found the girl he loved dearly. They
were married and lived in up-state New York. When his
little one was one year old, both went to Europe for a
vacation, visiting both grandparents; that was a great joy.
Prior to their departure they had their home phone
disconnected. When he returned alone he did not change
the status of the telephone because he was working
overtime where he had a telephone at his disposal. That
had been the end of July. Since we both had been very
busy, neither of us contacted the other.

It was a night in October ... I went to sleep as usual.
But very soon I came to life, I hovered in my brother's car
and constantly prodded and talked to him:
"Let me drive ... you know I am a safe driver ... and I
don't mind night driving ... let me take over the steering
wheel ... you are so tired ... you can hardly keep your
eyes on the road ... watch out, don't drive off the road
... come on, let me drive ... wake up ... don't drive on
the shoulder.." and more of the like.
But every so often I changed my abode and sat in an
airplane, circling over Shannon, Ireland, and seeing the
islands in early dawn, beautifully clear (at a time when I
had not yet traveled by air). Again I was back in the car,
and once more in the plane, but there was no rapport with
any one in the plane, the young woman at the window was
sullen and preoccupied. I had only seen my brother's wife
briefly three times before. Anyhow, I was mostly in the car

=151=

with my brother. Finally the horrid trip was ended safely. He parked the car in the parking lot, slammed the door and, I awakened. The clock at my side pointed to 10 minutes before 7 AM, the usual time for the alarm to ring. I stretched myself, and told my husband and child about the strange night with my brother. After the sixth time, my husband suggested I call my brother. I did, it rang, but no one answered; he plainly was not at home.

I forgot about my brother; I was busy designing clothes all day, and when I returned home I had to hustle preparing dinner, setting the table, feeding the dog, and helping with the homework. When my husband returned, I dished out the food and had just put the first bite into my mouth when I shouted:

"Ah, just now he is coming home." I got up and dialed his number, and it rang and rang, at least 17 times, but I did not think of giving up. Then someone fumbled with the phone. I repeated my **Hello** three times, and then it was my brother's voice: "Oh, it is you, Hildegard ... I could not reach the phone fast enough ... guess whom I have on my arm? ..."

I laughed, "your little one!"

"How could you know? ... You couldn't! ... I did not write ... How did you know the telephone was connected? ... I am still in hat and coat ... we just drove into the garage when the telephone started ringing."

"I know, you drove all night."

"Yes", he replied, "I left Owego shortly after 1 A.M., and I arrived in New York, at Idlewild Airport exactly 10 minutes before 7 A.M. I hurried to the reception desk and found that the plane was a half an hour delayed because of an unscheduled landing at Shannon, Ireland."

58: He who has no love remains in death

1 CORINTHIANS 12, 7-10:
"Each receives his manifestation of the Spirit for the common good. One man is granted words of wisdom by the Spirit, another words of knowledge by the same Spirit; one man in the same Spirit has the gift of faith."

One year later my brother's wife lost her mother, and decided to make the trip with her oldest daughter. It was at the beginning of June, and I had made reservations as soon as school was finished to do research in France.

Since the flights from the United States terminate in Frankfurt, the young woman with their grandchild had to travel over Stuttgart to Munich, and thus could interrupt the trip easily enough to say hello to the other grandparents without any extra cost. Telephone contact was made several times. But each time the young mother could not control her weeping; the two-year-old, missing Daddy and her familiar surroundings, cried also. Even though, she thought she'd stop even if just for a few hours. However, she never committed herself. Death to her was final, she was forlorn, and lacked the love and hope of Christ's promise.

On the 10th of June I awakened with the certainty that something would happen to my mother, should the young woman decide not to let the grandmother see her grandchild for a second time in her life! I contacted the travel agency to see if it was possible to fly to Germany yet this day, instead of one week later. "Yes, that will suit us fine ... for your seat next week we have a long waiting list. Can you report at the airport by 6 P.M.?" Next, I cabled my folks:
"Get things ready for me, will arrive from Luxemburg at about 5 P.M."

I owe my life to Jesus--You also?

The flight was considerably delayed, but I arrived safely by 9 P.M. Both my parents received me with great relief and happiness. But my mother called me by the young woman's name ... very strangely mixed up. I was led upstairs to the guest room with the childs-bed from the neighbors freshly fixed up.

Then my mother sat next to me on my bed, and she put three or four dolls she had made in my lap, and I played with them, musing her. 11 P.M. had passed; my mother was beginning to relax. She could laugh again at a funny tale. Finally, I took all the dolls in my arm and said to her: "Mumsy, don't you think I am a little too big for dolls?"

All of a sudden she opened her eyes and looked at me: "Oh heavenly Lord, it is you, Hildegard. Of course you are a "little" too old for dolls. I have been dreaming ... I had looked with such love to holding three year old Barbi in my arms, and Thea. Just think, she called me yesterday from Frankfurt ... still crying, and the little one crying, too. I was still on the phone when your cable arrived. Now I really thought, she and the little one had come afterall. Is'nt it sad."

1 JOHN 4, 13-16:
> **"We know we have crossed from death to life, because we love our brothers; he who has no love for his brother remains in death."**

The loss of her mother made the young woman hate all those whose mothers were still living: "Why must I lose my mother, such a saintly mother, at such an early age, not fifty yet, when other mothers who have lost their usefulness, are doing well at seventy!" Yes, it was very, very sad.

59: When Christ appears, you'll be with him in glory
COLOSSIANS 3, 1-5:
"Since you have been raised with Christ, aim at what is above, where Christ is, seated at the right hand of God; mind what is above, not what is on earth, for you died, and your life is hidden with Christ in God. When Christ, who is our life, appears, then you will appear with him in glory."

I had finished student teaching before Thanksgivings Day, 1963. The High School football team had won the game; a pep rally was in full swing. It was past the noon hour when I climbed into my car, a beat up V.W. without a radio, heading back to college. It was a bright and sunny day. I had the window down and my elbow resting on the frame. I entered the big loop leading to the gate of the turnpike. All of a sudden it struck me, I drove the car off the shoulder ... the motor died, and I sat in a trance. Then I heard the voice of Mrs. Kennedy come through exclaiming: "Oh my Lord, John, this is not worth it, this is not worth it." I saw men in white letting their hands sink, one of them asking: "Is he dead?" And after a pause: "Is there nothing we can do?" ... "I am afraid not."

Minutes ticked away. When I had rallied, I started up, finishing the great bend to the gate and said:
"President Kennedy is dead ... what happened?"
The man at the gate answered: "Oh no, he is not dead, they took him to the hospital to give him aid ... some one shot him, they just announced it over the radio."
"No, he is dead."
"Hope you are wrong, sister."
I shook my head and drove on.

We all remember the days that followed. Then school had picked up my full attention after the recess. I did not record the date, as nothing that I have written here was ever recorded, therefore, I do not remember whether it was the night of the second, or the third of November, not that it mattered to me then or now. But it happened nearly two weeks later.

I owe my life to Jesus--You also?

I have to stress that I went to sleep at the normal time, in the usual manner, and with exactly nothing on my mind, except for Christ to do whatever HE pleases, as is my habit, dead to the world.

Soon I was conscious of extraneous labor, indeed, I was not alone, there were many, many, many of us. Around us it was not really dark, but neither could I call it light. If it had been inside of a home, one would have called it subdued lighting. Here we all were standing at various levels on the slope of a murky pool, or a dense black cloud filling the hollow. We were gesturing, and also wringing our hands in frustration, hope and anxiety, all wrapped up in one, every one on his own. This is what I was saying, and what others said in their own way:

"John, we cannot help you ... it is up to you ... you must want it ... lift up your arms ... listen to us ... open your eyes ... see for yourself, Christ will meet you ... but you must want to meet him ... everything will be alright ... believe me ... believe in the Lord ... really, it is so easy, lift up ... reach for Christ's hand ... you must want it ... it must come from your heart ... Christ will give you eternal life!"

Slowly John's face appeared and one eye lifting; then his arms began straining away from the crossed position. At that I was turning toward the bright light shining down the sloping incline, the one I had hurried up when I was ten. Now I saw Christ, like I had seen HIM then, filling the full light, a towering figure. I ran with a few others up toward HIM to announce that it was time to come for John, that he was rallying. But Christ was not interested in us, with one sweep of his hand he cleared us out, wanting no witnesses.

That very moment I awakened in my bed lathered with perspiration from the genuine exertion. I was very happy that John had made it, even though the Lord did not want witnesses. It was about 5:45 A.M. I took a bath and was singing a Halleluja, I was refreshed as if I had overslept. This is what always amazes me, how one can be refreshed by sleeping, with Christ caring for and recharging the soul.

I have only witnessed these two resurrections, mine and John's. Accordingly, when Christ told the one criminal on the cross: "I tell you truly, you will be in paradise with me this very day," then HE meant just that. That person who honestly believes in HIM, whose soul has nothing to hide, and whose conscience is clear that he has done the will of God on this earth as best as humanly possible, him the Lord will meet at a flick of an eyelash. Others need prayers and, I suppose, intercessory laborers of love. My Mary did not need any one, and therefore I knew the very moment that her soul was free. I went along to the funeral, because of Chet and Mary's mother. On the other hand, John needed all the intercessory prayers he could get. His mind had been set on other matters, the choice of the hour had not been his.

However, this also serves us as a warning: be prepared for the Lord at all times. This does not mean that it will be easier if you just sit and wait ... one cannot shirk one's duties and responsibilities in this life. Walking with Christ from day to day, dying each night, and receiving a new lease on life each morning, can spark you on the way.

It is certain, we get a new body ... the best image we, ourselves, have ever aspired on earth, but were not able to attain. If we limped, or squinted, or had an ear which ever so lovely crooked, we keep that, too ... I mean those characteristics which identify **me** from any one else, for it is said: The Lord recognizes us all, and he calls us by our name. I know this to be the case. But remember:
We must want to meet CHRIST ... it depends upon our FAITH, and our LOVE.

60: Your time has not yet come

2 TIMOTHY 1, 3,7,9:
"I render thanks to God ... for God has not given us a timid spirit but a spirit of power and love and discipline... I am not ashamed of it; I know whom I have trusted, and I am certain that he is able to keep what I have up into his hands, till the great Day."

The Lord had kept HIS promise, I had my degree, and a choice from among five positions. I was asked for an interview by a church college where I could have had everything I dared to ask for: love, status, an open door for development, and a grant for faculty children to study where they wished. And yet, what the Lord had shown me, did not match anything I saw there. In retrospect, I know I was not meant for that position, for I would have enjoyed my days, and not developed as I had to under stress.

I went on to a State College where everything matched the Lord's picture. Here I was needed for a small group of students for church and school on Sundays. I had dear, dear neighbors; above all I loved my teaching job. I proved to myself that a good teacher did not have to mark time, wasting opportunities by not feeding willing minds. The feeling was mutual; the students loved me, and worked very hard. It was fun for all concerned. The Lord was with me all the way, including one year of incredibly beautiful weather.

During the fall I had a vision Sunday night to Monday: I was summoned to the bedside of my father in the hospital. My mother was sitting at his side wiping his forehead, talking to him and weeping. A nurse was working on him from the other side of the bed. At the head of the bed was a partition separating mother and father from another room. Behind the partition nearest to my mother stood a very modern-style record player. At the far end the door opened, and, not visible to my parents, my maternal grandmother entered with her slightly limping gait. She looked younger than I had ever seen her, blond, curly hair, wearing a beautiful flowered dress. Under her left arm she carried a record which she placed on the turntable, a beautiful requiem sung by "angel voices": "Komm suesser Tod..." (Come sweet death...), very familiar, reminding me of Psalm 90, 3-6:

> **"Age after age, Lord, thou hast been our home from all eternity, thou hast been God, ere ever the hills were born, ere ever earth and world were made. Thou crumblest man away, summoning men back to the dust, Thou to whom a thousand years are like the flight of yesterday, like an hour passing in the night. Year after year sowest men like grass that grows anew, that in the dawn is fresh and flourishing, then by twilight fades and withers. Come sweet death, that I may see..."**

Abruptly my grandmother broke off the concert, slipped the record into its jacket; taking it in her right hand she walked out a little faster than she had come in. It had been rapturously beautiful, and my mother had broken down weeping on my father's shoulder.

At this point I entered my mother's and father's part of the room with poise and confidence. I told my mother not to weep; I gave my father a hand, helping him out of bed; I laid their hands into each other's and led them to easy chairs side by side, telling them: "Look here, your hour has not yet come, joy will be yours, take heart: I will be with you in the summer." All tears were wiped away, and I looked into their sunny faces.

I awakened to one of the most glorious mornings God had created for me. The time was 7:15 AM, and about noon European time. The telephone was clamoring for attention. It was my brother from up-state New York. He was crushed and indecisive: "Hildegard, I have very bad news: it looks like I have to fly to Germany. I received a cable from mother to inform me and you that father has an intestinal blockage and is dying."

Without thinking, I said in a most joyful voice: "Thanks for the call, but never mind, Dad is going to be alright, you will see!"

He retorted: "From where do you have that? Did mother contact you?"

"No, not that ... you just wait, and you will see!"

By now he was bewildered ... angry ... frustrated, and slammed down the phone. All the same, I drove, singing the bewitching melodies, all the way to college, and thought no more about it.

On Thursday, about 5:15 P.M. after work my brother again called me. He had received a night letter from my mother: "Monday morning your father was rushed to the hospital with an intestinal blockage. The surgeon operated at eleven o'clock, by twelve he was back in his bed. By evening he could get out of bed and by Friday he is to be discharged for home." Then my brother added: "I still cannot see how you could have known that!"

At the time I had no intentions of returning to Europe in the near future. I had no inkling that by May I would be accepted as a Ph.D. candidate at the University of Basel and, of course, a joyous reunion with my folks.

61: You have been with me from the beginning
JOHN 15, 26-27:
> "When the Helper comes, whom I will send to you from the father, even the Spirit of truth who issues from the Father, he will bear witness to me; and you too are witnesses, for you have been with me from the beginning."

I gave exams early ... we had decided on using the Modern Foreign Language tests prepared for first and second level college German. No one, not even I knew what they entailed. I had an agreement with 85 students that the higher grade should prevail, the combined average, or the test score. No one stood to lose ... it was a challenge to see if they could improve their score.

I was proud of them, for they finished on a beautiful curve over 160, a high average nation wide! Every one was excited about the outcome. Meanwhile I had to find a place to store my household for the next two years. I assumed that it would be safe with faculty and parents of faculty members. After all, I was paying the going rent for the room ... I had no other alternative. To accomplish this I had many dedicated helpers. The last day came, my bags were packed and the grades were handed in. When I entered the classroom for my last class my students took over and sent me on my way with a lovely remembrance. Then they loaded me into a car with all my baggage and sped in a wild ride to catch the plane with hardly five minutes to spare.

At Newark everything had to be transferred into a waiting helicopter and from there reloaded into the waiting overseas plane. "Yes Ma'am, your baggage will be on the plane!"

Our plane was already warming up on the runway when a lorry rushed over with flashing lights. Moments later the breathless official tapped me on the shoulder: "Here are your vouchers, we found the three pieces, they are on board." He hurried back out and the plane proceeded down the runway.

I owe my life to Jesus--You also?

The Lord had decreed it, and this was the auspicious beginning of a seven year challenge with research, and of a 45,000 mile tour through Europe to find the homeland of Cinderella! I should discover that she was not just a poor pretty wench, but the kidnapped president of a "United States of Europe", North of the Roman Empire at the time of Julius Caesar.

To recount all the blessings and divine guidance during this period would fill a book by itself. But it may be said here: Without Jesus Christ I would have come to grief. In all the miles I had no accident. I met all the key people in the field; and won the enthusiasm and aid of local archaeologists, archivists, linguists, interpreters, and other helpers. I made hundreds of friends from Norway to Greece, including Hungary, Yugoslavia, Slovakia, Poland and East Germany. I let Christ worry about vacation schedules, absences and other details in scheduling my route. Where to find food, exchange, gasoline, the Lord was my guide for the entire course of events. Bit by bit I unraveled the mysteries of the ancient peoples. Even the weather cooperated; either the floods had dissipated before my arrival, or they innundated miles on end behind me.

In retrospect there is no end to HIS marvels!

Two years later I stood on the pier in Newark, the V.W. loaded with my things, and $5.- to my name. The man who delivered my car cheered me up; instead of putting just a thimble full of gas into the tank he filled it completely, and sent me off with God's blessings. I called my sister-in-Christ in Pennsylvania to let her know I had arrived safely, happy as a lark, but broke.

"Will you have me back?" That dear, dear soul ... I felt like a carpetbagger. I should not unload my car for a long time. I found a nursing case, an old lady to be in my care in an historic house in Philadelphia. There my car was parked in her empty garage. Her son and his wife were dear Christian people, deacons in His church.

I was home without a home, and yet, I was very blessed, because I knew that the Lord had plans for me, no telling where HE would lead me next.

=162=

62: Pierced by remorse confess your love

2 CORINTHIANS 7, 10:
    "...the pain God is allowed to guide, ends in a saving
    repentance never to be regretted, whereas the world's
    pain ends in death.

My father had enjoyed my brief visits during my stay
and research in Switzerland and Germany. Yet we were not
free to share as we would have liked. My mother had built
a devious wall around both of us, of partial truths and
misconceptions, which she wished to keep alive at all cost.

My father was fluent in English, so he resorted to
writing on empty spaces in the Time Magazine, and I
answered him in the same manner. The explosions from
ammunition and bombs during the first World War had
rendered him almost deaf.
    One day we were walking in the garden in a blustering,
chilly wind, when my father turned to me: "Don't try to
talk to me, I cannot hear it before mother has picked up
part of it, I can talk softly and you will understand me. I
am asking your forgiveness for having failed to do enough

to nourish your mind and soul. I tell you truthfully, I would have enjoyed it ... I should never have let mother hold the reins when you were little. You could have learned most anything!"

"Dear father," I wrote into his magazine, "You know in your heart, it is because of you that I am living. I knew you loved me, and I always loved you. I knew what kept you from doing more for me..." We both fell into each other's arms, and wept ... for the first time in 50 years, father and daughter. We had so much to tell each other, now it was too late; he could understand, but not hear. My mother's ears were everywhere; she could hear, but not understand. He loved her and depended on her, and she did her best. After twenty years his hip's plastic surgery had partially eroded, leaving a small wound which would not heal.

During the spring that followed, when I took leave, father brought me to the garden gate. I wanted to take him once more into my arms ... he would not yield. Instead, he stood forbiddingly at attention ... I knew then, what Mary had said in her wisdom: "Hildegard, no, don't come. You know too much!" He stood there for awhile like a statue, then he turned and went slowly back into the house.

I knew then in my heart that I should not see my father again alive on this earth. He had met his daughter as Christ had wished it.

63: Wherever the Spirit, open freedom

2 CORINTHIANS 3, 16-18:

"...though whenever they turn to the Lord, the veil is removed. 'The Lord' means the Spirit, and wherever the Spirit of the Lord is, there is open freedom. But we all mirror the glory of the Lord with face unveiled, and so we are being transformed into the same likeness as himself, passing from one glory to another -- for this comes of the Lord the Spirit."

I had taken a half-day off from duty to do some errands. It was a gray day in March, drizzling off and on. I looked at my watch, already 1:30 P.M.; I was driving briskly through city traffic when suddenly a cord in my heart snapped. I pulled out of the traffic, and I heard my father's voice calling my name:

I owe my life to Jesus--You also?

"Hildegard!" At that I breathed deeply, and completely changed my direction, heading for a travel agency. I said to the clerk: "My father has just died and I need an immediate flight out to Germany to be with my mother as I had promised him."

"Tomorrow evening at 5 P.M. is the earliest flight available from New York."

I began to write out the check, I looked up at the woman and apologized: "Tell you the truth, nothing has been confirmed, but I am expecting a telephone call from my mother."

"That is fine, we are open until 8 P.M. The seat is available; we will hold your check until we have your confirmation."

On returning I told the relatives of the old lady what had happened. "Call the hospital." I placed the call shortly after 5 P.M., person to person, either mother or father." The operator could not understand German, it was then 11 P.M. European time and I was switched to three different nurses, the last one informing the operator that my father had been "discharged" at 6:45 P.M. ... exactly 1:45 P.M. our time. I told the operator that the call could not be completed. I called the travel agency to confirm the reservation. Next I called my mother at home.

Mother answered right away; her life, everything she had lived for, was shattered. "He had strepto-septicemia, and was in a coma for nearly three weeks. He seemed to rally shortly after 6:30 P.M. late this afternoon; I had trouble understanding him, he was saying your name over and over again: "Lord, protect my Hildegard! ...""

I knew in my heart that my father was with the Lord ... he could hear again! One day we will be reunited in the Lord.

64: The Lord has dealt graciously with us

LAMENTATIONS 3, 19-23:
>"The thought of my stress and scattering is bitterness, bitter to me; my soul is always thinking of it, and is crushed within me... But I will call to mind, to give me hope, that Eternal's love is lasting, and will never fail. 'Fresh every morning is thy kindness, great is thy faithfulness!'"

My trip to aid my mother was ill-fated from the outset. The plane was prevented from landing due to a snow storm, detained in Brussels for hours. My mother was in a state of uproar and revolt. She was taxing herself with house cleaning. She fed the faithful tile stove anything and everything she thought useless (like the Time Magazines she could not understand). The temperature in the house climbed above 90 F. and was maintained. With her legs heavy with varicose veins, and a heart condition, she went up and down the stairs from morning till night. Even before the funeral had taken place, she had put the house up for sale: "Oh, those hated steps!" She resented help, and she did not wish to be talked to.

Memorial services had been arranged years before, and father's many friends had been informed. They came to pay their last tribute to a beloved teacher, comrade, and true friend; we were greeted by the larger family.

At the grave a day later, only my mother, my aunt and I were present. An official in a black suit was carrying the urn sanctimoniously before us to the grave. I had to think of the time when my father in ages past had talked to me about last things. We were sitting in the meadow of our garden overlooking the sun-filled valley. He used to say: "When I die my body is to be burned, and the ashes dispersed by the wind; who wants that old body! Flames? Nothing can touch the soul! My soul will be free and with the Lord. It cannot be otherwise, else all those blasted and obliterated by bombs would be condemned to forfeit eternal life, and the love of Christ!"

By now the official and we three had reached the grave; just as he wished to lower the urn its handle broke, it tumbled into the hollow, opening and spilling some of the ashes ... all that was missing was the wind. I could not suppress a chuckle. My mother did not take notice ... I don't know where her thoughts were, with her legs, with the task ahead of clearing the house? No, she set momentarily to the task of filling in the earth herself, and of planting as many flowers and bulbs on this bit of sanctified earth as it would hold.

My aunt, a very devout woman, had turned around and gave me a look denouncing me for being amused by this incident. Then watching my mother perplexed, as she was fussing with shovel and rake over the grave, Aunt Minna left us in frustration, and went to the grave of her beloved husband. There she remained in prayer until my mother was done.

Back at home, my mother turned against me like a steamroller. Finally she sent me down backwards three steps into the cellar. It was an unfortunate fall, I had torn ligaments internally. With last energy I crept to the car and signed myself into the University Clinic in Frankfurt. The Lord had removed me from being a target and placed me over Easter into lovely care.

When mother found out what happened, of course, she came out of her shock, and felt very badly. She took time out to pay me a visit, which at her age was really a full day's trip. She had to negotiate busses, trains and streetcars. She had arrived in good spirits. However, homeward bound, she missed the step into the train, slipping over it, hanging there with one leg between the platform and the track. Her legs were badly bruised, and she was taken to a nearby hospital not far from home. This I did not know. When I came home, I found her upstairs in bed, forlorn, without care and food, still unable to negotiate the steps in her house.

During the 18 days I was in the hospital mother had found a buyer. She had already opened an account in my brother's name at a bank so that she could deposit the proceeds from the property as soon as settled. She was frustrated; now she could not procede to sell or move. My father's account was frozen, his will not yet probated, and she had no place to go. The next three weeks became an endurance test for me. I was still shaky from the surgery, and my stay enormously expensive, because I had to drive endless miles in a rented car to find a suitable place for her within her means.

Finally I had to leave for the States without accomplishing anything, except by virtue of my presence, serving as a catalyst for the accumulated hatred, pent-up over nearly fifty years. (It was not necessarily directed against me alone, or caused by myself, but I was the only one there.) I grieved sincerely for having lost my father, mainly because with him I lost the last vestiges of what I had called "home" on this earth.

The Lord had dealt graciously with him and with me. HE had given him a lease on life for 20 full years, since coming to the States, 30 years since the day the physician discovered the inoperable cancer, and 52 years since the Lord spared his life from the hell of Verdun during the First World War. He was in his eighty-sixth year of life, with full memory, still teaching Greek and Latin, English and French to students wishing to pass entrance exams at Universities!

Psalm 150: **"Hallelujah! Let everything that breathes praise the Eternal! Hallelujah."**

65: Never grow tired of doing what is right

NEHEMIAH 1, 11:
"Ah, Lord, may thine ear now be attentive to the prayer of thy servant ... Ah, let thy servant have success at this time, let him find favour in the sight of ... man!"

I was welcomed back on my nursing case with much love and understanding, as well as with relief. I settled down to my routine. My dear sister-in-Christ was very, very ill; my prayers hovered over her day and night. The Lord heard our prayers and gave her a new lease on life.

In August, while on the job, I had a vision: "I had a teaching position in the capital; I saw myself steeped in research at the Library of Congress; I saw myself typing my book on a typewriter system not yet developed. I met my partner, one deeply interested in collaborating in my research and the book. Somehow I wom the esteem of my son, so he would turn to the Lord, and the two of us were again showing our love for each other."
In this vision many things about me were different. I wore a different hairdo, very becoming and making me look years younger; I was high-spirited and happy; I wore sharp pantsuits (styles which did not appear on the market until 1977). The vision went on to show me being accepted at various universities for my research, receiving my Ph.D., and being welcomed as a guest lecturer, here and abroad.

This vision overawed me. What a window into the future ... it filled me with wonder, amazement, and hope! Most of it seemed humanly impossible to attain. Life in the capital held no attraction for me. Seats of government attract corruption, unethical, devious characters to lobby for a multitude of causes. As a student of ancient history I was not yearning to become a part of a faceless crowd to live off the scum of society. That may seem harsh and callous, but the minority in government today are God fearing men. In 1968 no respectable woman wore pants. I had no writing skills at all. I had no prospect for a teaching position, although I had signed up with three agencies. I was convinced, however, that doing research was in line with my abilities.

Already on the following day I received three job applications from an agency, which I answered immediately. One of them answered by telephone, asking me to come for an interview. I accepted the offer.

As I drove, I realized that Outtown College was was within reach of the Library of Congress. However, during the intervening year I found little opportunity to do research at the Library of Congress. One year later received a call to Downtown City College. Was that the college the Lord had meant for me?

House-hunting was an other story. I attempted to find a place close by. The first time I thought I had found a place, I walked around the block to check the neighborhood. When I returned to my car, I found my typewriter gone. The second time, I found that the apartment building had no freight elevator and my furniture would not fit in the available one.

That was the way I came to settle in Virginia where I made many friends. There right in my neighborhood I also found a new Church Home. In a sharing circle I learned to think and talk about the gifts the Lord Jesus Christ had given to me, and no one thought it funny or queer. For once I was not alone, but with a group of believers.

Praise the Lord for His mercy! Lord, bless them and keep then in YOUR LOVE!

66: Any realm divided comes to grief

MATTHEW 12, 25-27:

"Any realm divided against itself comes to ruin, any city or house divided against itself will never stand; and if Satan casts out Satan, he is divided against himself; how then can his realm stand? Besides, if I cast out daemons by beelzebul, by whom do your sons cast them out? Thus they shall be your judges. But if I cast out daemons by the Spirit of God, then the Reign of God has reached you already."

Was Downtown City College the college where Christ had wanted me to teach? ... "Yes, unequivocally!"

With a few exceptions, the students were underprivileged and ill-prepared to do college work; they were older than the average college student. It was a challenge to devise ways of providing them with a foundation on which to build a successful future. High school and transfer credits were paper dragons, which had to be ignored. Assignments had to be spelled out, and supplementary material had to be made available. Work habits had to be established, and an English vocabulary to be built. Diction and spelling had to be a part of the course requirements. Above all, the student had to become involved; he had to be shown the mechanics for developing independent thought and opinion. The students, when left alone, loved my classes. They discovered quickly that they could apply my guidelines to other courses, realizing that they held the key to their future.

To teach bright but underprivileged students takes special skills. Above all, it requires a teacher who masters the material to be taught, for he needs all the freedom to explore new avenues of meeting and leading the student. Once rapport was established the student absorbed every-thing like a thirsty sponge, and worked for himself like a beaver before nesting. What a joy to watch!

I owe my life to Jesus--You also?

Downtown City College had no student problems, the difficulties lay with the faculty. The faculty was divided, one half deviously imposing their laws on the other. The faculty was divided ... "any house divided against itself will never stand", a handful of leaders left riot-swept Plaintown University and set up housekeeping at Downtown City College. Since then Plaintown University had had peace, but riots engulfed D.C.C. Subversive elements streamed to Downtown College from California and Boston by invitation to give these new faculty members a hand. They participated freely in faculty meetings, where they served as cheer leaders and hecklers. Their prize event was the instigation of the "Outtown College Incident". Big Bill, the Department Chairman, outlined the goal: to divide the administration and render it ineffective. They voted for the third president, because they thought they could manipulate the man. When this proved wrong, because the man was in Christ with integrity and honor, the battle was on.

Another honest man headed the library; he was also to administer the purchase of a language laboratory. The henchmen formed their own purchasing committee; I was to be the third person. We were to inspect several systems put in by the same firm, one of them at Plaintown University. There he introduced me to his former department with a flourish of words, but those very people turned on his outstretched hand and evaporated without a word. "You know the way to the Lab, Bill," was their icy reply...

Big Bill sent his children to a private school; he shared a Mercedes, he bought a big house and had it redecorated, brand new furniture on order, a new four digit High Fi system, he wore elegant suits, and he implicated the head of the Library for embezzlement of funds, ruining the man's health and career.

Big Bill had himself nominated to become the first staff member to join the Board of Higher Education, as advisor and to negotiate with the board without consideration of the incumbent president. Between them, the henchmen covered

=173=

the key positions within the college. They played havoc with the records. They used the students of Downtown City College like the Nazis used the German people. If they could not be coerced, they hired trusted outsiders to serve as stooges. They planted these in all the classes of faculty on their black list. They helped the stooges write complaint letters and took them unchallenged to the President and the Board as proof of student protest. Some of these protest letters had less than 5 signatures. No one investigated or verified whether even these few signatures belonged to students registered in a class of that particular teacher.

Transcripts of those faculty members Black and White were conveniently lost, to impress the Board that he had to be dropped for lack of "qualifications" to teach in a college. On the other hand, unqualified staff members were represented as working hard to remove their deficiencies by being enrolled in graduate programs. What they did not say was "how long", "how unsuccessful", or "where". If nothing else would do, they would enrolled them in a program in Downtown City College itself.

To witness, they did away with my graduate records faster than I could supply them. To save themselves the embarrassment they finally did away with my whole file. Members of the group served as terminals for the "underground railroad" from Haiti, leading via Canada, giving them their first employment at Downtown City College, if nothing else but as student assistants. For deserving students no funds were available. This was detrimental in general for the willing student, for these people had an utter lack for the educational needs of the American student, or of an inner-city person.

The College suffered from chronic shortage of paper. Writing tracts for purposes such as advertising the "Outtown College Incident", was a heavy drain. They were involved in the riots at the University of Suburbia, for which the particular students and stooges took a holiday from classes. They had briefings at the office of the Latin at least once a week.

=174=

I owe my life to Jesus‑‑You also?

In staff meetings they propagated the idea that black students could not by nature perform as well as white skinned students. They admonished the staff to be indul‑ gent with their habits of absenteeism, and non‑compliance with the assigned material. However, the absenteeism in the classes of the perpetrators often exceeded 80%, while in my classes 5% was a high percentage. In general, Satan had a field day, dividing the house. The lack of paper was a handicap. The elements invited stole large and small pieces of equipment, even the computer‑check‑out counter for the new library, typewriters by the dozen, and audio equipment. In the visual‑aid department taping of the worst kind of porno material was going on, to which language lab tape was diverted. Miles of these must exist. Obstruction went deeper: funds were cut or allocated to deprive the students of essential facilities like the reference library, and a substitute language lab which I had set up to facilitate my students, supplied and graciously supervised by the voluteer Library staff. I had provided most of the tapes out of my own funds and had made the recordings on my own time. They broke the camels back by cutting appropriations for two student assistents so they had a reason to close the facilities for working students.

One of the henchmen held a law degree. He was a gay, giving freely of his expertise in legal matters. He used to "study" Nazi techniques of harassment at a neighborhood library I frequented at the time. He admitted openly to having planted stooges in my classes, and unrestrictedly threatened me and others with copyright suits, libel suits and legal action.

Hard as they tried, they could not find cause to fire me. Therefore they decided to change tactics to induce me to resign voluntarily. For awhile they organized harassment calls during the middle of the night. They dwindled when I began to answer them, sending greetings to the instigator by name.

=175=

Then they tried to do away with me altogether. First they had me identify my car, and next they sliced my tires badly. I was unsuspecting. It was high noon, May 11. I was on the Beltway in the outside lane ready to pass slower traffic at 50 mph. There was a loud explosion and I was heading for an open space to be hurled to Henneticut Avenue below. I let the wheel go and said aloud: "Lord Jesus, here I come!"

"Oh no, you are not," HE replied, "take the steering wheel and carefully turn it to the right, like so ..." The car leaned against the concrete guard rail and was propelled back onto the highway. From then on the Lord was in charge:

"Take your hands off the steering wheel!" I complied. I did hardly know coming or going! Would I turn over? The Lord said: "See the dotted line? Take the steering wheel and hold it to the line and pump the brakes as much as you can ... pull the wheel toward the left enough to keep traction." Again I leaned against the guard of the bridge head, this time in the middle. Again I was spun onto the pavement in a wild zigzag, ordered to take hands off the wheel, again HE showed me the dotted lane demarkation. HE put my hands on the wheel and made me pump the brakes until I slid against the guard rail for the third time, this time at the very end of the overpass. Once more the Lord took my hands off the wheel, letting the car do what it pleased until the white dotted line appeared. This time the Lord made me hold the line as long as possible, braking in short pumping motions. The car felt much steadier; but alas, it curved again to the left with too much speed. Again there was a bridge guard to lean against, this time over Komptown Parkway. The car swung back onto the pavement once more. The Lord commanded hands off the wheel, and when the white demarkation line appeared HE made me steer the car in a shorter curve to the left pumping the brakes harder. I hit the guard on the other end. The speed was broken, though the car bounced into the traffic lane until I saw the dotted line; I supplied just enough tension to keep the car rolling, 10 mph., then 6 mph. I was nearing the

=176=

shoulder, 2 mph., then I approached the grass with 1 mph.
It followed a short dragging, a dull plunk, and I sat with
the left side in a rut off the shoulder. During the whole
maneuver my briefcase never slid off the seat.

A car stopped behind me, while I was still thanking my
Lord. I could barely open my door wide enough to get
myself out. A man came hurrying to my side: "Are you
alright? My God, you drove as if with angels! Let me take
you in my arms." That felt really good. Then he held me at
arms length. "I heard and saw the blow-out. I was behind
you but in the slow traffic lane. I went immediately behind
you to cover the lane in case you should roll, and block all
the traffic. Do you know that you never left your lane? Do
you know you never really hit the guard rails?"

A policeman joined us. He looked at my beautifully
"parked" car and said: My, oh my, you must have driven
as if with angels! Every other person would have taken off
and flown right through those bushes and into the
on-coming traffic ... Let me summon a wrecker ... you
know, you'd make a good stunt driver!"

When the wrecker lifted the front wheels the trooper
suddenly exclaimed: "Look at that! Do you know you blew
two tires? Do you know you had no tires on the driver's
side? And you still managed to ride out the car from 50
mph.? ... Setting it down safely like this? Let me touch
you ... by the grace of God."

Indeed, the men had said the truth, I drove with
angels, with Jesus Christ at the steering wheel! I felt hot
and cold inside, I was happy and very, very thankful. With
the Lord at my side I could face anything.

I owe my life to Jesus-- You also?

67: God's children in a crooked and perverse generation
JEREMIAH 7, 19; 7, 8-9:

> **"Spite me?" says the Eternal -- "they are spiting themselves, bringing shame on themselves! ... You are relying on false phrases, to no profit. What? Steal, murder, commit adultery, perjure yourselves ... thinking you are now quite safe -- safe to go on with all these abominable practices!..."**

By January the minority at Downtown City College swung themselves into the driver's seat. They had successfully ousted 44 faculty members, Whites, and those Blacks with intelligence and integrity. Students became prey to their mandatory politics if they wanted to graduate.

So far, my classes had been a great success, arousing even more jealousy. In January a stooge was planted into a large class with a tape recorder. He was a man of 33 years, a stevedore, not officially on the roster; he signed in on the sheet with the late comers. The classroom assigned to me for 30 students had no windows. Overhead the ventilator control grill had been removed and the hot air streamed in unrestrainable. The room had an average temperature between 90F and 102F. After each class the stooge returned the tape recorder to the chairman of the department. When his performance failed to improve, a brief check unfolded the whole picture.

A petition was written on a typewriter of **the Judge** to the president in the stooges behalf to have me fired for incompetence. This letter was hand-delivered to the Board of Higher Education. Between writing and delivery three weeks of hard soliciting elapsed during which some 80 students were hard pressed to sign it or leave my classes. None would sign it. The president asked for my presence, and declared that the charges were insufficient and invalid. None but four stooges had signed.

One morning I was met by my students in the hall: "We cannot get into our classroom; the door is locked, and we are unable to locate the key."

I owe my life to Jesus--You also?

That information, I assure you, was very accurate. Over night the door was provided with a second Yale lock above the original one. As I walked back through the hall for help, I walked right into the arms of the Dean, talking with a student.

"Don't you see that I am speaking with a student? ... Oh, really, by now you should know that I have nothing to do with the Department; if you have a complaint about a classroom, you must take it to the Department office!"

In the Department office sat a recent arrival from Haiti employed as the new secretary, speaking little English. When I returned to the classroom, the Department had planted two stooges in front of the locked classroom, preventing late students from reading the note posted on the door announcing the new place for meeting of my classes. The students were told I had quit teaching.

The classroom was sealed for two weeks. Then I took matters in my own hands. The registrar, and the head of the housekeeping department were furious, and did not believe me. He sent a man up to investigate ... sure enough, the door had a new lock. He called me back: "Who has the key?" I visited three offices. The culprit was not to be located. I found some clues and passed them on. Within two hours the door to the classroom was opened, sporting a hole where the lock had been. This maneuver had split the class in half, from 28 to 14 students.

During the following staff meeting I made a brief report about the incidence. The Dean and member of the Board of Higher Education, grinned to the recording secretary of the Faculty Organization, a competant woman, with a Haitian passport. He said to her under his hand, shrugging his shoulder my way: "Did you? I knew all along in whose pocket the key was!" She smiled and nodded her head.

The Dean invited me for a talk in his office: "Mrs. Lotz, you see, it is very difficult to teach in a place like Downtown City College, first of all you don't belong in this institution."

"What are your reasons?"

He began to stammer: "IF I~I~I ww~were yyy~you, I~I~I w~w~would bb~be ss~so ashamed, s~ss~so ashamed ...", he invaded my living space waving his index finger precari~ously close to my nose, "ss~so ashamed ..."

"For what reasons should I be ashamed?"

"If I-I-I were ww~white I ww~would bb~be ss~so ashamed tt~to ff~force mm~myss~self into a bb~black inss~sti~tu~ss~sion like DD~Downtown CC~City C~k~k~ollege."

By that time he was right on top of me. The Dean himself was light milk~coffee color. He was too close, without touching my nose. Words would be out of place ... I left his presence. Behind me he raised his voice: "YY~You ss~s~see, you will not even let the D~D~Dean of tthe CC~College tt~t~talk ww~with yy~you k~k~kalmly!"

Satan was at work dividing the house, hoping to live off the spoils. The Dean was not interested in building up a college, serving the students, or the Black community of his city. He was frittering away precious opportunities in order to exploit racial tension; in doing so he did away with precious resources and time.

I filed a complaint with the E.E.O. counselor. Knowing the situation full well, he accompanied me himself to the city headquarters. The case was approved to proceed to the Court.

Meanwhile my counsel was prevailed upon to drop the hard line. For one year four of his college-age children had a very difficult time. They flunked out, and could not find employment. Once he had given in, all that changed over~night; they were back in school, or in a job. Then the judge slated to handle the case was persuaded by "circum-stances" to let a fellow judge, a friend of the Haitian and the Dean, handle the case. The first concession they won was the elimination of a jury. The deposition was made by a clerk who could neither handle stenography nor English. The deposition was never honored.

The Judge dragged out the trial over two weeks. Right from the start the Judge intimidated the counsel and myself. False exhibits were in order without recourse. The testimony of the witnesses really did not matter at all.

When the whole thing was over, my counsel buried his face in his hands and muttered: "The only decent thing left to be done is to declare the entire process a mistrial." He added, **"but leave me out!"**

At the door, the Counsel for Downtown City College called over mine comfortingly: "Max, don't feel bad about losing this case, you have the other one, you know, we will let you have that one. You can be sure, because most of it is already admitted, we know where we stand from the beginning!"

I asked at the beginning: "LORD, was this truly the college, YOU had intended for me?" Again I must answer without hesitation: "Yes, unequivocally."

I used my time wisely and with utmost discipline. I spent two summers abroad on research; I put in twenty or more hours per week at the Library of Congress. I signed up for 24 credit hours of graduate work at the Uptown University, fulfilling the residence requirements for the Ph.D. in a second field. I lined up my research project. When they took away my classes by threatening the students with failure in other fields, AAUP upheld my contract, and they paid me one year without assignments. This was the year I used to finish up my research and write my historical novel, working without exception 12 hours per day.

The historical novel is to be a pleasure for the average reader, its title: "A Woman for President". It tells about the original historic setting of **Cinderella** in our Fairy Tale. She was not a poor, pretty wench, but the PRESIDENT OF A UNITED STATES OF EUROPE, who was kidnapped and held in exile under hard labor for 14 years. Her story is preserved in an old manuscript in the archives of Vienna. To discover and safely identify the territory and her home state, I traveled over 45,000 miles criss cross through Europe in a V.W. camper. I was able to find much more evidence than I could have dared to hope. It shows brave women upholding the integrity, faith and honesty of statesmanship. To complete the research without a mishap was in itself a chain of miracles. I encountered no accidents or health problems. The court affair could not harm me regardless of the outcome. I had filed as the pauper I was. The financial burden was on the tax-payer of the City.

The whole experience, however shows clearly that "any realm divided against itself comes to ruin." That no good can come of educators and judges worshipping Satan.

"The Reign of God" has not yet reached the United States, either. I do not feel singled out, I cannot be harmed by Satan and his advocates, for Christ is ruling my life. That is why I spelled it out. This is to encourage you, Black or White. Be steadfast, oh you children of Christ.

Would I teach again at Downtown City College? Yes, any Day! You see, it was fun to see the students develop and grow, winning surety, confidence, and self esteem in valid achievements. All our institutions need a new Spirit to feed mind and soul of those entrusted in their care. Only that way can each new generation build on solid rock, and produce a single-minded, dedicated faculty, intent and able to do the very best in teaching.

Because of Downtown City College I accomplished much of what the Lord had promised me in the vision at the nursing case. In any other position I would have spent my energies otherwise. **HE is still the LORD!**

I owe my life to Jesus-- You also?

68: Heal the crippled and lame, I commission you
2 CORINTHIANS 6, 11-16:

"O my beloved, I am keeping nothing back from you;
my heart is wide open for you. 'Restraint'? -- that lies
with you, not me. A fair exchange now ... Open your
hearts wide to me ... what business has a believer with
an unbeliever? ... For we are the temple of the living
God -- as God has said 'I will dwell and move among
them...'"

I was looking for a home of my own in Virginia near my
church; one after the other I had signed three contracts to
buy a house, and each time I came hours too late. Then I
took one look in Maryland and loved what I saw. However,
it took almost 9 months before I could move in (April 1973).

I found two elderly people in need of a nice place and
care. One room I had for some one temporarily until he
could move into his own home. Come what may, I knew that
the Lord was with me all the way.

My church in Virginia was too far away, therefore I set
out each Sunday to another church, until I wandered into
the fellowship circle at St. Paul's, and my heart rejoiced.
During the four years, every one of those Your children,
Lord, grew in faith and in the confidence that YOU are
walking with each of them. May you feel confident that the
Lord will walk with you also! May HE pour out HIS love and
blessings upon all of us!

One Sunday morning before Easter we were sitting in a
circle as was our habit; the subject under discussion:
Should parents spank their children? Richard was saying a
prayer over his parents: "If I would not have had those
dear folks, I would never have gotten off the ground. I
would get a well earned spanking once in a while and be
told: 'yes, you can move and do what you are assigned to
do.'" Richard was a movement-handicapped, whose
childhood and teens were marred by the inability to move
properly. The group was not promulgating **spanking**, but
we were pondering the problems parents are facing in
trying to bring their children up in the Lord.

=183=

I owe my life to Jesus--You also?

While Richard was talking I had a vision, and the voice of the Lord told me: **"You have learned to habilitate cerebral palsy victims, go and help them to become normal! Listen to me, Your Lord! There is no effective program anywhere to prevent crippling. Be confident and of good cheer!"**

I was dazed for minutes, and then I said aloud to about 20 or more people: "Do you know what happened to me right now? I who have no license whatever in the medical field! It is ridiculous to think that the Lord should pick me, of all people! I have just now received a commission from the Lord. I am supposed to be the only one on this side of the ocean to eliminate CEREBRAL PALSY!"
"Well, write up your proposal, I'll help you with the English and I will see to it that it gets into the right hands at NIH," said Sophie.

I was quite excited ... but I must confess, that in all my training with movement-handicapped babies and their habilitation the word, "cerebral palsy" had never been used, not even once. Here I stood at 50 plus years, commissioned by the Lord, yet with no concrete idea of what CEREBRAL PALSY was about. I prayed, and in a vision by night the Lord refreshed my memory about all the steps and techniques I had learned years ago in Berlin.

Now it also became clear to me, that all along I had helped many parents to overcome the handicap and in this country, too, I had helped quite a number of parents. However, in every case I thought, those parents somehow had been singled out, for unknown reasons neglected, and thus exposed to the fate of seeing their child crippled. It had never occurred to me that in this land of progress nothing effective was being done to **prevent** CEREBRAL PALSY ...
I lost no time in researching all about CEREBRAL PALSY! C.P. (for short) is just a nomenclature given to individuals who are contorted, twisted, and lacking a muscle system strong enough to support a skeletal frame. Since twisting and contorting does not become evident until the baby is about two, the medical profession simply

=184=

assumes he has no C.P. until then. It is not on the books for under age one. No wonder that I did not know what C.P. was!

Next I went to the N.I.H. and the AMERICAN MEDICAL libraries, and researched everything which has been done in the field of Cerebral Palsy on this side and on the otherside of the Oceans. I found that the Lord was right. It could be read in two afternoons.

Most all of the cases come to the attention of the physicians long after the parents have detected the handicap, the movement disability. This is a crime ... it does not have to be that way. All babies are tested for their ability to move **at birth,** and any movement disability **must** appear on the hospital form which accompanies the birth certificate to the state. When the baby, however, is dismissed from the hospital, this information is not passed along to the pediatrician or the parents. By the time their baby is three months old most parents begin to realize that one or the other limb, or none wiggle or move. The doctor cannot find an organic cause. Often those babies develop so normally and look as beautiful as if they lacked nothing at all. The spastic type gets much more attention, because of the spasticity, but **not** because of their inability to move. Unfortunately they often receive drugs to inhibit the spasticity and therefore reduce whatever chances for developing the muscles even further. Drugs in themselves cause additional damage in those parts of the brain still functioning normally!

Because of the space age, I found much background information as to why my method was successful and can be applied in all cases, and for all ages. I also learned why all other methods had to fall short of the goal: **complete habilitation.**

I began to write letters and tracts, making trips to see people in high places, including members of Congress. I spent 100% of my earnings, living on borrowed money. I let parents of movement-handicapped children know I could help their child. My church friends suggested I see the pastor for permission to put something into the bulletin. The pastor was afraid to pray before he knew what it was that I wanted, and afterwards he had to be reminded ... he was in a hurry. Several weeks later I received a letter from the church, signed by the pastor and three of the leaders of our charismatic group. The Church could not permit me to let folks know that there was help for C.P. The Church was afraid of liability suits for advocating medical aid. Since I was dependent on some income from it, the Church could not subscribe to a **commercial venture.**

One of the gentlemen who had signed was most outspoken about my "commercial venture". Some days later he approached me about helping him distribute a religious newspaper to augment my finances!

The Cerebral Palsy Association was approached on all levels. They were very candid: "Thank you for your proposal, but frankly, **if it truly would work, we could not consider it, because we have spent billions of Dollars for our programs ... we could not jeopardise all those jobs!"**

This was also true of the March of Dimes. The organization fought the introduction of the Salk vaccine for polio ... even fighting it in Court, until a judge threw out the case after 1 year and a half, as against the interests of the American people. March of Dimes did not collapse, but had to change its field of concentration.

The Lord's program is not dead. In fact, it has expanded to include all non-progressive handicaps like accident victims, quadriplegic or paraplegic, stroke victims, residual polio victims and spina bifida cases. None of these need to lie prone for the rest of their lives, or limp. There is no need for operations, braces, crutches or wheelchairs.

Two million of such people are waiting for help ... many thousands are hidden away in back-rooms, in institutions, nursing homes, and mental institutes.

If you are in search for help, for yourself or for a loved one, here is your chance: Included is an envelope and information. If you know someone with such a need, tell him about the good news. It's not a miracle **cure**. It is a fun program, and hard work for the whole family for the duration of one whole year ... like training for the Olympic games. It works, and it is permanent! If it is a baby under two years, it isn't even a chore!

The wisdom of the Lord is immeasurable!

69: Have faith: Teach parents to heal their lame!
1 CORINTHIANS 14, 1-4:

"Make love your aim, and set your heart on spiritual
gifts. Especially on prophecy. For he who speaks in a
"tongue" addresses God, not men ... he who prophesies
addresses men in words that edify, encourage, and
console them. He who speaks with tongues improves his
own lot; whereas he who prophesies improves the lot of
the church."

Water Gate had taken its course and Nixon has gone the
way I had prophesied in 1967/8 before his election. In
August I had a vision of war and disaster in the Holy Land
... I wrote a ten-page paper to President Ford, as I was
ordered: "Do not treat Israel as if a State of the United
States! It will ruin our economy and render the Dollar
worthless!"

We, who are standing for freedom and self-determination,
how dare we supervise the evacuation of 90% of the
population and see 90% of a new population move in without
recompense of the former? Dare we to expect God's
blessings? What, if a super-force would clear 90% of us out
of Maryland and resettle it with American Indians?

May the Lord have mercy upon us! The Lord said to me:
"Israel is so small that one atomic bomb will cleave the
mountain from East to West and end all of the endeavor!" I
hand-delivered it to the White House, and that was the end
of my duties. Ford probably never saw the paper. He never
comprehended the situation.

Again fall came around: I was working on my research
when the telephone rang; some one needing a room until he
would find a place to settle his family. It was the only
place he looked at, and so it was decreed from the
beginning. For the first three days we hardly crossed
paths. Then he said: "I saw your paper on the kitchen
table, I am very interested in what you are doing, I too
have researched in archaeology and ancient measurements."

"That is great, I could use a computer engineer to help
me figure out the mathematical side of the relationship of
the ancient German mile and the Greek and Mycenean foot,

the formula is set up already." Then I added, "Right now I am writing a paper on habilitating cerebral palsy victims!"

"Oh, that interests me very much for I have a little granddaughter with cerebral palsy."

That Sunday I brought him along to our church, where he felt right at home.

The Lord could not have placed a more beautiful person in my house! Out of nowhere Christ had picked a person who had done a good bit of research in the same field as I. He had no one to share it and I, too, had done everthing by my lonesome self. Now we could fill our limited spare time exchanging notes. He proof-read my novel. I wrote my research papers, and he made the corrections. He encouraged me not to forget about "project cerebral palsy." I continued writing letters and contacting various agencies and people about it. Then I issued a news letter and spent several hundred dollars for paper and stamps ... it did not matter. It seems that the parents are satisfied with having a cripple in the house. At least I did not hear a response.

My Christmas had been a very happy one. On Christmas Day I was late turning in as usual. That night I had a vision: The Lord was taking me to task on habilitating movement-handicapped in general and cerebral palsy in particular. At the time I had resolved to forget about it, and had become involved with other research.

Thus speaketh the Lord: "I have given it to you to rehabilitate non-progressive movement-handicapped of any age not just babies."

I answered: "Lord, I don't know whether I can do that, I am not strong enough to handle grown-ups, but if you teach me, I probably can do that, too!"

That turned the night into a workshop. First HE showed me the long line of those of all ages I had already helped at one time or other. Then HE put two little people with cerebral palsy before me, one spastic and one motionless. HE took one arm and said: "What must be done to restore life into this arm?" ... I showed HIM what I knew.

"Verily, what prevents you from doing the same on a grown-up person also? ... What must be done to this leg?"

I owe my life to Jesus–– You also?

Limb by limb the Lord rehearsed absolutely everthing which had to be done to make them look like normal. The Lord gave me reasons for everything. By the time I awakened I still heard myself saying: "Of course, dear Lord, I can do that with grown–ups just the same."

I was very excited and could hardly wait to share my new–found confidence with those who had movement–handicapped in our neighborhood. One family came with their partially afflicted ten year old. The doctor had not given them any hope: "Your daughter is now in a period of rapid growth which will wipe out all the gains she may have made."

Growth, or no growth, it worked and she became visually stronger and straightened out. Then the local health service department threatened the child and the parents to cut off all state health services for the child if they dared to seek help from private sources. I went to the State Health Services in Baltimore to find out about the official policy.

"As long as a parent is present, any one can teach the parents or the child anything they wish, including habilitation for non–progressive movement–handicapped. No office of the State can deprive any one of state aid of any kind, as long as the person has been declared eligible." The local authorities had intimidated those dependent on them, the damage was done.

The parents' response was evasive, or like the following: "Well, it is inconvenient –– truthfully, we are **satisfied** with the progress our child is making at this point. We are **afraid** to lift our hopes too high. After all, **we** have to live with it. Never mind, we have to trust in our doctor, he ought to know what he is doing and what can be done." Braces, operations, wheelchairs, what a pity, if one could do very well without!

I talked with the doctors: "Yes, what you offer sounds great, but I cannot get involved, for among my patients I have only one, or two and it would not be worth my while to concentrate on researching the merits of your course just for those two cases!"

I owe my life to Jesus--You also?

By Easter my house guest had settled in his own home with his family. In August his daughter brought his little granddaughter for a three week visit. Melinda is a typical random C.P. She has had all the conventional treatments since she was three months old. At five years she was badly twisted, and weighed hardly more than 14 lbs. The mother was very skeptical as to the value of efforts, but since her father and her brother were willing to pitch in, she went along with everything. Two days later her attitude had changed. By the third day progress was evident: her little girl began to blossom under all that attention. After the first week her muscle tone began to improve and she was able to lift her face off the blanket, turning it from side to side, bracing herself on her elbows.

After the second week she began to eat as if starved. Two months later she weighed 18 lbs. By the end of three weeks she was just about straightened out. She could close her mouth by herself and fought for head-control. If she could have stayed another three months, we could have helped her over the critical period. Unfortunately, the mother did not get assistance at home to continue the necessary routine. Nevertheless, we know that Melinda can learn to walk within a year if she were given a chance under this program. As long as her mother continued working on her she gained weight to 24 lbs. Since then a year has passed at the prior pace, now she does not weigh more than 26 lbs. Skeletal growth robbed Melinda of all the advantage she had had. It was so much fun working on her. One person alone cannot do it.

There are 750,000 cerebral palsy registered in the United States alone. Each year 110,000 new cases of spina bifida are born; there are as many stroke and accident victims. Wouldn't you like to help? Won't you spread the news? Thank you Lord for prodding us to lend a helping hand to those who cannot move!

If you do, there is a need for those who cannot afford to hire outside help, or to pay the one time fee of $600.- Please send your requests and/or your contributions to Crippled, Box 27, Linthicum Heights, Md. 21090.

I owe my life to Jesus--You also?

70: Rejoice, Your names are enrolled in heaven
LUKE 10, 1, 17-20:
> **After that the Lord commissioned other seventy disciples, sending them in front of him two by two ... The seventy came back with joy... "I have indeed given you the power of treading ... down all the power of the Enemy; nothing shall injure you. Only, rejoice not because the spirits obey you: REJOICE because your names are ENROLLED IN HEAVEN."**

For many years I have gone to the same church and to one Sunday School class. For the past years, in addition, I enjoyed listening to two sermons each Sunday on the radio. Now I have changed my pattern, true!

Lowell, you asked me, whether I am spreading myself thin? Frankly, I had never thought about it. If the question pertains to loyalty, I can answer you joyously: "I am loyal to Christ, and to his flock!" I have nothing to spead thick or thin; I have the need to consolidate. I know I have much to offer, but I am as gregarious. I let Christ lead me, for HE knows what I need and who is offering just that. I have never felt regret for joining a fellowship, or a service. The Lord's ways are strange and wonderful, and there is no end to the diversity and beauty of HIS children.

To be a disciple of Jesus is not meant to be difficult. He touches you on the shoulder and says: "Come follow me." Then HE says: "Open your ears and listen to ME, try to understand what you are hearing."

Discipleship entails first **to follow Him,** and secondly **to be HIS pupil,** thirdly, to become **HIS student.** A child follows his mother ... the new-born are "typed" to know to whom they belong. Some of us are thus typed to know that Christ is with us. To follow Christ, luckily, there are no prerequisites. Then you learn about the free assurance plan for eternal life.

A pupil is to listen and to learn as well as to ask questions. He is either fed graded material, or he is

=191=

absorbing only as much as he is ready to understand, depending on his maturity. He is to learn and memorize as much as possible to pass the tests of life. As a follower of Christ he grows into new capacities and usefulness as he learns to use his new found skills. Being a pupil, and then a student, however, implies that eventually there is a graduation, after which one has to enter **an apprenticeship.** That means, that no one but the master is monitoring you, HE HIMSELF is giving you the assignments.

Question: Who has to work harder to learn and understand, the teacher or the student? If he is a conscientious teacher, he works twice as hard. For it is easy to be a student especially when spoon-fed. It is another matter to master the material so you can feed it bit by bit without losing sight of the whole.

And after the apprenticeship some of us
are commissioned to go in front of HIM two by two.
With this fourth step "our" problems truly begin. What then were those commissioned to do in front of Christ? (Matth. 10; Luke 10)

1. They were to announce HIS coming, preparing the people to receive HIM.
2. Enter a household and bring Christ's peace.
3. Decide whether there was a SOUL, and IF there was a SOUL breathing peace, give him Your peace, it will rest on him, if not, it will not be wasted and come right back to you.
4. For doing a good job, you are entitled to due wages. On entering any town, eat what is provided for you, accept hospitality.
5. Heal those who are ill.
6. Tell them "The reign of God is nearly on you."
7. If you are not received by a community you are to tell them that their very ground and all it contains will fare worse than Sodom and Gemorra.

This means, therefore, nothing more and nothing less than that those commissioned were on their own. They were to do a multiplicity of tasks in Jesus' name in new and changing situations. All I can say to you: Please be patient with me, God is not done with me yet!

71: I believe in miracles

MATTHEW 14, 14:
> "Jesus saw a large crowd, and out of pity for them HE healed their sick folk."

You are asking me: "Do you believe in miracles?"

"Yes, the other day I set out to cross a six-lane highway. Having crossed two lanes my motor died ... a dead stop! A car I had not seen whizzed past the nose of my car shaking it from air pressure. My motor sprang back to life, and my car vacated the two lanes to make room for the on-coming traffic which I had seen before. Yes, **Yes, I BELIEVE IN MIRACLES.**"

You are asking me: "Do you believe in the resurrection, in a new body, and eternal life?"

"Yes, I believe! Not only do I believe, but I am positive, for I have experienced what it will do for us."

You are asking me: "Do you believe in healing?"

I owe my life to Jesus--You also?

"Yes, I do! By the fact that I am alive and able to sit here and write, is the best proof of it! That my dear father was able to attain 86 years of age is proof of what the Lord's healing hand can do! That my dear mother is still alive in her 90th year, not-with-standing a bad heart condition since she was 35 years old, is that not proof enough? That my dear brother was on the last lorry leaving Stalingrad, that he was sent out of headquarters before the bomb hit, and was able to raise his three children despite severe kidney operations? These are miracles, miracles!"

Well, I know this is not exactly what you are asking me. "Yes, I do believe in healing. I believe that Christ has commissioned his disciples to go and heal the sick." Truthfully, it is easy to answer you ... it makes me feel like a hero. But when my COMMISSIONER asks those very questions I wish I could evaporate in thin air. I hear myself saying: "Yes, dear Lord, I believe in healing." Though I am very quick to add, "but I am swamped with so many other things, I had better leave it up to YOU." The Lord has HIS ways.

I was busy typing my book; it was a Saturday, and I expected 12 or more guests for supper. They were to arrive by 6 PM. Before I became stiff at the typewriter, I took time out for cleaning; at 10 AM I was working in the bathroom. A small glass had a stain inside on the thick bottom. I held it in my left, and bore down into it with my right. How was it possible? The glass slipped off its base, and the rim dug itself to the bone over the heel and the first joint of the thumb. I lifted the mess off my hand, and said out loud: "Lord, why do you let such a rotten thing happen to me! You know I have no health insurance; no income to pay a doctor to sew this wound together! And even if I did, I haven't the time to go after one. I haven't even the proper materials in the house to dress such a wound like this ... with only one hand! My house is not cleaned, my guests are coming, and I have to be able to finish typing ... now this? My blood is running away like a river, and ..."

I owe my life to Jesus--You also?

My beloved, to tell you the truth, I had to do something. I shut my mouth and listened for counsel. Then the voice, a little fading voice, of the Lord asked me: "Do you believe in healing?" --"O.K., YOU heard my answer: Yes! But now YOU better make sure that all the glass-splinters, if any, are washed out," thereby I held the mangled hand under the free-flowing water. I pulled the thumb toward the palm, added some nose drops to all the wetness, and plunked cotton on top of the cut. Then I found a roll of narrow adhesive tape from yesteryear, and wound it over the whole palm and thumb in such a way that the wound could not gap. Then I said to the Lord: "Very well, what I have done is common sense, now You'll have to see me through this day, and leave me with enough spirit to enjoy my guests and the music they are coming to make!"

Truly, I tell you I had not so much an ache or pain because of it. I was as busy as I had planned it, I carried chairs, finished the cleaning, cooked the meal, did everything, as if nothing had happened. I don't think my guests were aware of what had happened, or why I wore the bandage. I did not look at the wound at all. Why? It did not hurt.

On Tuesday evening I was at the automat-self-cleaners and the girl attending, a student nurse, said: "Your bandage has had it, would you let me make a new one?"

I looked at it ... she was right! "No, it is healed: when I get home I will take it off." It was healed beautifully, just as it had felt all along.

Shortly later my mother had a series of heart attacks and I asked a group of the Lord's faithful to lay hands on me to heal her, and to ask the Lord for forgiveness for me and for herself. The Lord let me see her lying in bed waiting for her blessings and going to sleep peacefully.

I was with Dick when he collapsed passing kidney stones. I was with little Ester in her crisis over a period of three days until its passing on a Thursday afternoon. I was with Howard, Jim and Al when they underwent surgery. Not that I learned to schedule a special time for prayer, but I earnestly told the Lord to remind me to pray that He should guide the hand of the surgeon HE had selected to aid them (at the right time).

Here is what happened with respect to Howard: I was on my way to New York with a friend to see the headquarters of March of Dimes on behalf of my movement-handicapped project. We were sitting in a Motor Inn for breakfast, talking about this and that. Suddenly I put down my fork and said to her: "Howard is on the operating table; let us pray for him." At the same time I saw in a vision exactly what the surgeon saw and did, when he was finished he straightened up, satisfied. Then I looked up at my friend and said: "I am sure Howard will be alright!" Later I checked the hour and it was indeed the very minutes which were critical.

With Jim ... I was in the kitchen on the telephone all morning. I had finished one call and was about to make another, when I put the telephone on the hook and said out loud: "Oh yes, dear Lord, let us be with Jim (open-heart surgery)." I stood in my kitchen, and my soul was out of my body. Again I could see what was going on through the eyes of the surgeon ... it lasted perhaps as long as 15 or 20 minutes of physical time. When I could breathe again I knew that Jim was mended. I think I called his wife right away and told her that Jim was fine.

With Al it was a similar experience during his first operation. When I called Olivia, I knew her husband was to be with the Lord. In like manner I sustained and was myself sustained by my beloved Aunt Johanna until her 96th year of life just a couple years ago.

Yes, I believe in healing. Yes, I am commissioned to heal those that are afflicted with cerebral palsy, and other movement-handicaps. However, **those sick must want to be healed, and must believe in the Lord healing them!**
Praise the Lord for His mercy and love.

72: Anything can be done for one who believes.

MARK 9, 23-29:

> **Jesus said to him: "If you can"! Anything can be done for one who believes. "And the father of the boy cried out: "I do believe, help my unbelief." ... He said to the disciples, "Nothing can make this kind (of evil spirit) come out but prayer and fasting."**

To be commissioned and sent ahead of the Lord is at best disconcerting, especially when you have no partner ... probably that is the reason why Christ always sent his disciples two by two. But I truly feel no different from any of the seventy. Every time I have gone "out" healing, I returned to the Lord aglow with a happy heart, saying: "Lord, the very daemons obey us in your name."

And the Lord said: "Yes, I watched Satan fall from heaven like a flash of lightning. I have indeed given you the power of treading on serpents and scorpions and of trampling down all the power of the Enemy; nothing shall injure you."

And I interrupted the Lord saying: "I guess, I've earned another gold star in heaven!"

I have run into a person possessed by the devil. Praises to Jesus for the providence that I was not alone ... HE sent our Sister Ester with me. It was on a Sunday morning between 8 and 9 A.M., we came with a lighted birthday cake; the door wasn't locked. The fight and the struggle which ensued was fierce, and encompassed the poor woman as completely as Mark 9, 18-27 describes the boy who was brought to Christ. The monster attacked me with all the means it had at its disposal. No part of my body was spared. The battle lasted for almost two hours when the unclean, deaf and evil spirit left the body of the poor one. A completely limpid, meek and exhausted child, she was finally able to sip a swallow of coffee Ester offered; we led her to the couch, exhausted.

=197=

I owe my life to Jesus-- You also?

Ester and I covered her up and we prayed with her, then we tiptoed out for church. That was when I began to realize my state of exhaustion. I wept and prayed all through the service. The Church had out-of-town guests, and wished to celebrate a common meal of delicious soup with all the congregation, and Ester and I needed help for our sister. Nothing but prayers and laying on of hands would help ... now or never.

I was led downstairs, still in shock. I was seated in their midst and we all prayed, until I could see the girl lying on the couch, the blood pulsing again through her veins, drifting into sleep. Then my heart was comforted, and I knew that the Lord had heard our prayers and would never, never let that evil spirit touch our sister.

Despite ice and snow and sleet, I looked after that child of Christ three times a day and made certain that she had what she needed, love and food. She had lost her voice completely. At last she was strong enough to drive to work, even though without voice. On Friday noon my phone rang: "I can speak again, you are the first one to know ... thanks!"

I was sitting in the tub filled with hot water. My body, after a week, looked like a Piccasso in black, green, yellow, and all shades of blue. If that was all the damage ... the gain was infinitely greater. I believe it when Christ said: "Nothing can make this kind come out but prayer and fasting."

Should you ask me: "Can you cast out evil spirits?" I will answer you honestly: "No thank you, that is not down my line ... but I know I will not run."

Two years have passed since, and many more years are to come ... I am confident that our gain is permanent. We claimed her to be the child of HIM, who is OUR LORD and REDEEMER. Amen

I owe my life to Jesus--You also?

73: Take courage, you are mine!
ACTS 18, 9-10:

--And the Lord said to Paul in a vision by night, "Have no fear, speak on and never stop, for I am with you, and no one shall attack and injure you; I have many people in this city."

The significance of the Bible consists not in the scriptures, but in the fact that it has been entrusted to down to earth people like you and me. What good would it do us if Paul, for instance, had been an exceptionally outstanding person? A person who always knew what to do? Look at the verse above: Paul was scared ... Paul was not sure that he was saying the right thing; he was scared to open his mouth ... Paul was alone in his decisions on the spot ... Paul was afraid for his life, and the crowd ... Paul dreaded the idea of being wounded ... Paul was not sure that in continuing he was doing Christ's will. Would he find a backing by the fellowship of a congregation. To do whatever he was doing just to prove his heroism, was out of the question. There had to be more to it than for the glory of his own person. After all, he knew that his name was enrolled in heaven, therefore Paul did what he did to win souls for Christ.

It all boils down to this: Paul was humanly speaking "in a stew and a pickle"; he did not know whether he was coming or going. Otherwise **the Lord did not need to appear to him to say the above!** The Lord gave Paul confidence, self-assurance, companionship, freedom from care for his own safety, preservation of his health, and the certainty of victory! Who can't move mountains with that, if Christ is with him all the way?

How long must an individual be a learner of the word? How long his student days? The eleven had by far the longest instruction period of all. The Lord commissioned the seventy (or 72) after a much shorter period; and Paul HE commissioned in a week. In other words, Christ has ways to instruct us on the job. The criteria is our **readiness,** our maturity, and our willingness to accept the call. Accepting a call takes courage and faith in one's own ability, the worthiness of the goal, and the faith in the one who commissions you. But you become guilty by not accepting

=199=

just the same! Don't forget that!

Look back on your own life. All of you reading this have graduated one time or other from one level to another, and some of you from college, and few of you with the highest attainable degrees. You all know the wonderful feeling of having made it at graduation: your family glowing with pride, you are thrilled. You are in seventh heaven, if on top of all this glory, you have a letter in your pocket to start a new job for pay on Monday morning.

By Thursday, three days in the new job, you are cut down to size. If, at graduation you felt like a hero, on top of the mountain with nothing more to climb, and the world at your feet, now you realize that the mountain you climbed before was nothing but a small hill. Your boss expects you to show him how you can climb the bigger one on your own. There is no one to blame, no excuses for lessons undone, no one to correct mistakes, all glaringly evident, if the boss should look in your direction. In real life, human beings can go to any length, and expend any amount of energy to cover up ... WATER GATE! My College episode!

No matter what your office, no matter how humble your vocation, **if you are commissioned by CHRIST you simply cannot cover up anything!** Instead of wasting your resources and your energy on cover-up, you are to use the same amount of energy to do your best to stand on solid ground. How can you be sure you are right, and the others wrong? How was Paul sure he was right, and not just a rabble-rouser? Christ reassured Paul ... Christ reassures you and me! **Christ is not crucified and dead!**

If it were otherwise, the DEVIL would have the field, the Black and White **BIG BILLS** would have it, and the Bible would never be written. NO indeed! **Christ is living, and walking with me and you,** and HE knows when you need HIS reassurance in the same measure as Paul needed his in Corinth.

So much for Paul, I know for a long time that the Lord has commissioned me. It was not easy. For instance, HE had commissioned me to write the historical novel. As a novice in writing, HE sent me the right teachers. I learned to type, and to be patient, writing each page four times or more. I succeeded remarkably well.

I owe my life to Jesus--You also?

While the market is seeking slush and trivia, to be apple polishing, to whip up excitement in sex and vice, and wanton killing, the novel has other goals: to make people more wholesome in their thinking and aspirations. For a Christian book the novel does not sound appropriate, because it deals with an era before Christ had walked the earth. Then why would Christ commission me to write the novel in the first place?

Despite its complexity, the answer is quite simple: The Lord wished me to learn to deal objectively with people ... how else could I deal with them in my novel? Even the most vile characters on earth are loved by some one! The Lord wished me to resolve resentments, and to understand all phases and dangers of bias. HE wanted me to understand what it means to obey HIS COMMANDMENTS. Above all, HE wanted to teach me self-respect, and give me a joy that passeth all understanding, an inner strength: for our body is **his temple** on earth. Who then has the right to defile it? With this gift, the Lord said: "I have indeed given you the power of treading ... down all the power of the Enemy!"

What does this mean: "Let the dead bury the dead?" ... "Wipe the dust off your feet?" ... "Turn the back and curse?" ... "If there is no soul, your peace will return to you?" It means that the Lord taught me to resist evil characters where I found them, upholding HIS LAWS, and facing up to my responsibilities; to use my energies for the betterment and salvation of my fellow men.

Since a historical novel transcends present nationalism, but has its own, the Lord took me on a 45,000 mile journey across the face of Europe, behind the Iron Curtain ... not as a tourist. I lived with the people, and experienced their problems of everyday life. My experiences as you have seen, sickness, hunger, mental depravation, poverty, fear, terror, anxiety, excitement, hope and fulfillment, peace and love, were absolutely necessary to let me deal justly with the people standing behind the historical events described in my novel. Any novel if it is to be worth its salt, is to a degree autobiographical; that holds true for mine.

You will ask me: if that is true, then Christ has to be also in your novel? Of course the Lord is in my novel! Does not St. John 1, 1-5 and 14 say:

> The Logos existed from the very beginning, the Logos was with God, the Logos was divine. He was with God in the very beginning: through him all existence came into being, no existence came into being apart from him. In him life lay, and this life was the Light for men: amid the darkness the Light shone, but the darkness did not master it ... So the Logos (the WORD) became flesh and tarried among us; we have seen his glory -- glory such as an only son enjoys from his father -- seen it to be full of grace and reality."

Does not Revelation 1, 8 say: "I am the Alpha and the Omega," saith the Lord God, who IS and WAS and IS COMING, the Almighty."

The Lord is in my novel, for HE lived with the Father before HE walked the earth. The only difference between those people and us now is that they did not know his name; HE had not revealed himself in the flesh to them, and therefore they called HIM the "Great Unseen." On the hill of the Court in Athens where Paul spoke stood monuments to all Greek gods, and also one to the Great Unseen (or Unknown), to the Spirit which guided these peoples including all their other gods. Just as I could not possibly have survived on my own, my heroine could not have survived either without HIS GREAT SPIRIT.

To do justice I had to experience the heart aches brought about by the corruption of LAW, the big Water Gate, and my little one at Downtown City College I had to know the "peaceful" conditions behind the iron curtain, and I had to be persecuted in my own home by the Heon Gang shouting over the fence one day on hearing me sing a praise to Jesus in my back yard:

"We will teach you something else, and then see whether your JESUS, JESUS, JESUS will help you!"

Yet, the Lord's peace remained with me. When I could not manage alone, Christ has sent me you, his faithful to help me out of the pit; or Jesus appeared to me at night, saying:

"Have no fear, write on and never stop, for I am with you, and no one shall attack and injure you; I have many people in this country."

Book Review:

I Owe my Life to Jesus -- You also?
Willyshe Publishing Co., Inc., Box 27, Linthicum, Md. 21090
$11.95 (45c handling), pp.210, 36 illustrations.
-- Author: H. Winky Lotz

If anyone has doubts about the presence of Jesus Christ in today's world, let him/her read **I Owe My Life To Jesus -- You Also?** Mrs. Lotz through her personal accounts and witness to the power of Jesus in her own life, may well provide the reader **a key** to the unlocking of his/her life to the reality of Jesus in the 'here and now'.

Mrs. Lotz's use of Scripture as the springboard to her sharing of life experiences, was to this reader one of the highlights of her book. Many of the passages came alive right before my eyes. This reader has studied Scripture and read many exegeses of given passages, yet for the first time I feel I understood fully what the writer was attempting to say.

If there is one criticism of the book, it is that it might not appeal to the average "Christians" filing into the pews on Sundays. It is a sad commentary concerning these individuals who feel that going to church on Sundays makes them <u>Christian</u>, for they will not be freed up enough to feel the presence of Jesus throughout this book, as revealed through Mrs. Lotz's life sharing experiences.

But for the non-Christian, or the non-institutionalized Christian who is looking for valid solutions to war, race and sex discrimination, drug abuse, just to mention a few of the many social ills of our time, they may find the inner strength through Jesus Christ to continue the struggle to return God's World back to God.

Annapolis   The Rev. Norman D. Crews
September 6, 1980

I owe my Life to Jesus--You also?

May 30, 1980
Excesses of alcohol, drugs and smoke destroy the human being, and the best of families. All wars are conceived by the adversary. Dealing in weapons bears a curse.

Trust in Jesus Christ is essential for survival in this day and age. Jesus sustains us in any situation.

This book sets an example, and gives the reader encouragement and renewed vigor. It is a great witness for the living Lord. V.M

July 12, 1980 The unique and interesting style and word usage serve to point up most vividly the reality by which the author perceives; the core of the book points at the way she sees Jesus Christ intervening in her life.

Mrs. Lotz has created a unique statement of religious belief as it can exist in today's world. C.P.

July 15, 1980 Unique and meaningful to me; it never had occurred to me that race, sex discrimination and parents' bias could be transferred at a very tender age. Religious education of our very young children should be pursued much more seriously and must become meaningful. Churches are encouraged to defer social and benevolent activities, instead do a better job teaching Jesus Christ and the word. J.O.

July 16, 1980 That a person loses his life, is declared dead for hours on end and is returned to life led by Christ himself: "Your time has not come, your father is waiting." But to have other experiences and to be able to convey them, is rare. It truly encourages the reader to trust in the Lord; to become more dependent on Christ himself. J.Ch.

About the Author:

H.Winky Lotz has published this book "I owe my life to Jesus -- You also?" as an encouragement to all those who are seeking as she is, for the truth. Is Christ a figure of the past? A mere matter for remembrance? Or, has he risen and is alive, and we directly responsible to Him for our daily actions?

Why does healing work for some people and not for others? Some churches are very effective; why are others not?

You all know when you believe, or "wish" to believe in something. Talking in tongues is fine when you don't know what you want. It clears your mind of preconceived ideas. No one has seen God, many have seen Christ, all feel the Spirit. Why not give them a chance?

Look at the centurion, the father of the one possessed by the devil, the woman who touched Jesus' robe -- how many others had daily contact with Christ? Why did it work for some, while others rubbed elbows with Christ, yet nothing happening? Faith like love, is either complete or non-existing. We can fake it, kidding everyone around us but not Christ.

H.Winky Lotz has traveled extensively throughout the U.S.A. and Europe, on research or lecturing. She is an acclaimed member of the Toastmasters International. 1975 she founded the Maxi-Move Institute for healthy movement-handicapped, an effective (1 year) self-help program for the home.

In addition to this book she has published two historical novels: "A Woman for President," shedding light on an era in which women headed a powerful Federation reaching from Iran to Norway. The 2nd volume explains the roots of our fairy tale heroine, **Cinderella.**

Other top selling Publications by H. Winky Lotz
and the Willyshe Publishing Company

1 **A Woman for President**, Foundation of the Federation of the Goths,
   stretching from Iran to Norway. (B.C. 175 - 95)
   ($14.55 plus 45c postage & handling) This is a historical novel based on
   real to life people ... brave women who were the heads of government,
   used to delegating jobs to men for which they were better suited. Women
   are less susceptible to bribes and corruption than men, and less easily
   persuaded to make war. Maps, ills.

2 **A Woman for President, The Roots of "Cinderella" of Our Fairytale.**
   ($14.55 plus 45c postage & handling) A historical novel B.C. 95 - 55 ...
   women heading the government, created a unified structure in law and
   legislation which was to last for 600 years or more. It deals with a
   president, whose fate is remembered in our "Cinderella Fairy Tale". Women
   have more integrity and are less corruptible, therefore better suited for
   high offices in government.

3 **The Maxi-Move Manual for healthy movement-handicapped**
   Individually structured physical fitness course. Membership required.
   Duration: 1 year. **This is no medical program.** A self-help home program to
   do away with the handicap of cerebral palsy, spina bifida, accident victims
   of all ages. Permanent help ... NO braces, no operations! Exercises are
   applied by the family.

4 **I owe my life to Jesus -- You also?**
   (7.95 plus 45c postage & handling) Charismatic, and autobiographical ...
   written to encourage you in faith, and to be willing to give Christ a
   chance in your life. An incredible account of faith and survival, beginning
   at age one, to the present. A must for the clergy! Jesus knows no race
   barriers, or male or female ... let's act like HIS children!

5. **"I owe my life to Jesus -- You also?"**
   Beautifully bound Library edition, 11.95, 36 illustr., 210 pp.

— — — — — — — **How to order** — — — — — — — —